# Teacher Edition

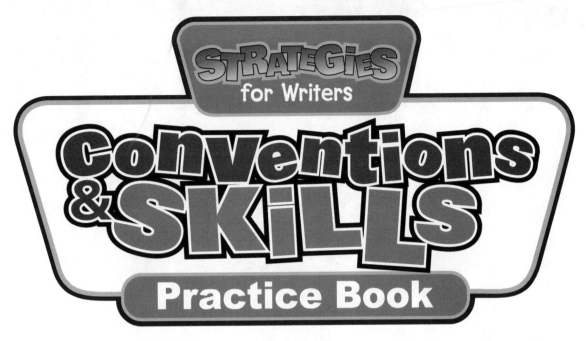

**STRATEGIES** for Writers

# Conventions & SKILLS

## Practice Book

### Level E

## Authors

**Leslie W. Crawford, Ed.D.**
Georgia College & State University

**Rebecca Bowers Sipe, Ed.D.**
Eastern Michigan University

**Editorial Development by** Cottage Communications

**Cover Design by** Tommaso Design Group

**Production by** Marilyn Rodgers Bahney Paselsky

Copyright © Zaner-Bloser, Inc.

Zaner-Bloser, Inc., P.O. Box 16764, Columbus, Ohio 43216-6764 (1-800-421-3018)

ISBN 0-7367-1259-3

Printed in the United States of America

02  03  04  05  06   MZ   5  4  3  2  1

# Table of Contents

## Unit 1
### Sentence Structure

## Unit 2
### Parts of Speech

## Unit 3
### Usage

## Unit 4
### Grammar

# Unit 5
## Mechanics

# Complete Subjects and Complete Predicates

## Learn

a.                                    b.

Spanish soldiers | built forts across the Southwest.

Which part, **a.** or **b.**, of this sentence tells whom or what the sentence is about? _____a._____

Which part, **a.** or **b.**, tells what happens? _____b._____

> Every sentence has a subject and a predicate. The subject of a sentence tells whom or what the sentence is about. The **complete subject** is made up of a noun or pronoun and words that tell about it. The **complete predicate** is made up of a verb and words that tell what the subject is, has, or does.

## Practice

Draw a line between the complete subject and the complete predicate.

1. Work on the Spanish forts | took over 200 years.

2. Adventuresome trappers and hunters | crossed this frontier after 1807.

3. They | sought valuable beaver skins.

4. The early Spanish settlers | created a commercial center in Santa Fe.

5. The Santa Fe Trail | reached from Missouri to New Mexico.

6. Mexico | owned both Texas and California.

7. Texas | won its independence from Mexico in 1836.

8. The independent Republic of Texas | became the 28th state nine years later.

9. The United States | challenged the British claim to Oregon.

10. The United States and Britain | agreed on a boundary in 1849.

Create a sentence from each group of words. Add either a subject or a predicate. Write **S** if you added a subject. Write **P** if you added a predicate. Remember to begin each sentence with a capital letter. **Sentences will vary.**

11. blazed a trail to the West ___S___

_____

12. Spanish soldiers ___P___

_____

13. braved the unknown ___S___

_____

14. sold beaver skins in the East ___S___

_____

15. fought many bitter battles ___S___

_____

16. the Republic of Texas ___P___

_____

17. Santa Fe ___P___

_____

18. a powerful Mexican army ___P___

_____

19. settled in the new land ___S___

_____

20. The British claim to Oregon ___P___

_____

# Simple Subjects and Simple Predicates

## Learn

SS                    SP
**Each state of the United States** has its own flag.

SS       SP
**These flags** remind us of the state's history or ideals.

The complete subject in each sentence is in boldfaced type. Write **SS** over the most important word in each complete subject. Write **SP** over the verb in each sentence that tells what the subject did.

> The **simple subject** is the most important word or words in the complete subject. It is a noun or pronoun and tells whom or what the sentence is about. The **simple predicate** is the most important word or words in the complete predicate. It is a verb. It tells what the subject is, has, or does. It may also be a form of the verb *be*.

## Practice

Circle the simple subject in each sentence. Underline the simple predicate.

1. Missouri's (flag) includes the same colors as the U.S. flag.

2. (Soldiers) in the Civil War often carried their state's flag.

3. Their (loyalty) to their states was very strong.

4. The (colors) on the Texas flag represent bravery, purity, and loyalty.

5. The Latin (motto) on West Virginia's flag means "Mountaineers are always free."

6. (California) adopted its flag with the grizzly bear and single star in 1911.

7. The state (tree) rises in the center of the state seal on the Florida flag.

8. The (shield) on Oklahoma's flag honors the heritage of the Osage.

9. (Ohio) flies a non-rectangular state flag.

10. A state (flag) always flies below the national flag.

Add words to each simple subject and simple predicate to write a longer, more complete sentence. Remember to begin each sentence with a capital letter and end each sentence with correct punctuation. **Answers will vary.**

**11.** flag flies _____

_____

**12.** states have _____

_____

**13.** United States uses _____

_____

**14.** artists design _____

_____

**15.** banner waves _____

_____

**16.** colors represent _____

_____

**17.** symbols mean _____

_____

**18.** guard folded _____

_____

**19.** soldier saluted _____

_____

**20.** wind blows _____

_____

# Compound Subjects and Compound Predicates

## Learn

Settlers and farmers in 1802 wanted the use of the Mississippi River. ____SS____

France controlled the river and exercised great power over its use. ____PP____

Write **SS** next to the sentence with two subjects.
Write **PP** next to the sentence with two predicates.

> A **compound subject** has two or more subjects joined by the conjunction *and* or *or*. A **compound predicate** has two or more verbs joined by a conjunction.

## Practice

Draw one line under the simple subjects in each compound subject. Draw two lines under the two verbs or verb phrases in each compound predicate.

1. Thomas Jefferson and James Monroe wanted the territory west of the Mississippi River.

2. They could take the land through war or offer money for it.

3. For 200 years, Spain and France passed ownership of Louisiana back and forth.

4. England defeated the French Navy and controlled the seas.

5. Napoleon and the American minister to France discussed the sale.

6. Jefferson offered Napoleon 10 million dollars for New Orleans and Florida and waited for an answer.

7. Napoleon needed money and wanted to sell the whole territory for 15 million dollars.

8. The purchase doubled the size of the United States and started a great westward migration.

9. States or territories were soon formed in the newly purchased land.

10. New Orleans and St. Louis became bustling centers of trade.

 **Apply**

Combine each pair of sentences to form one sentence that has either a compound subject or a compound predicate. **Answers may vary. Possible responses appear below.**

**11.** Steamboats carried goods down the river. They returned with new products.

Steamboats carried goods down the river and returned with new products.

**12.** The poor sanitation conditions in New Orleans bred disease. Open drainage ditches made things worse.

The poor sanitation conditions and open drainage ditches in New Orleans bred disease.

**13.** The Mississippi River frequently flooded the city. This destroyed wharves and leveled buildings.

The frequent Mississippi River floods destroyed wharves and leveled buildings.

**14.** A system of levees was built in the 20th century. This finally controlled the river.

A system of levees was built in the 20th century and finally controlled the river.

**15.** Cotton was the basis of the New Orleans prosperity in the 19th century. Sugar was also important.

Cotton and sugar were important causes of New Orleans' prosperity in the 19th century.

**16.** Louisiana was named for a French king. St. Louis is also named for a French king.

Louisiana and St. Louis are both named for French kings/a French king.

# Direct Objects

## Learn

President Thomas Jefferson wanted knowledge of the newly purchased western lands.
He asked Lewis and Clark for help.

Draw a line under the word that tells what Jefferson wanted. Draw two lines under the words that tell whom Jefferson asked for help.

> The **direct object** is the noun or pronoun that receives the action of the verb. Only action verbs can take a direct object. In a **compound direct object**, more than one noun or pronoun receives the action of the verb. To find the direct object, say the verb and then ask "What?" or "Whom?"

## Practice

Underline the direct object or compound direct object in each sentence.

1. Lewis and Clark knew the frontier and its dangers.

2. Congress approved $2,500 for the journey.

3. Lewis and Clark laid their plans carefully.

4. They explored the Missouri River and the area around it.

5. Lewis mapped the area.

6. Their party included 14 soldiers, 9 frontiersmen, 2 French boatmen, and a servant.

7. On July 30, they held a meeting with Native Americans at Council Bluff.

8. Later they hired a French explorer and his Native American wife, Sacagawea, as interpreters.

9. Sacagawea carried her baby boy on her back.

10. After 18 months, they finally saw the Pacific Ocean.

**Apply**

Complete each sentence by writing one or more direct objects. You should add other words to make the sentences more interesting, too. **Answers will vary.**

**11.** In May of 1804, Lewis and Clark began their long _____

_____ .

**12.** The explorers built _____

_____ .

**13.** To be successful, the expedition needed _____

_____ .

**14.** After many months, they spotted _____

_____ .

**15.** Lewis sent several _____

_____ back to St. Louis.

**16.** Congress supported the _____

_____ .

**17.** Earlier traders and trappers had reported _____

_____ .

**18.** During their journey, Lewis and Clark discovered _____

_____ .

**19.** The Native Americans provided _____

_____ .

**20.** These explorers gathered valuable _____

_____ .

# Indirect Objects

## Learn

Flags often send the **viewer** a strong **message**.

Write the boldfaced word that tells to whom a message is sent. _____viewer_____

> An **indirect object** is a noun or pronoun that comes before a direct object.
> The indirect object often tells to whom something has been given, told, or
> taught. It tells who or what was affected by the action. Indirect objects
> appear only in sentences with direct objects. To test whether a noun or
> pronoun is an indirect object, try moving it after the direct object and
> putting the word *to* or *for* in front of it.

## Practice

The direct object in each sentence is in boldfaced type. Underline each indirect object.

1. The wreath of olive branches on the U.N. flag shows the world a **sign** of peace.

2. The flags at the United Nations give all member nations special **recognition**.

3. The United Nations provides its members certain **privileges**.

4. A nation's flag gives people **pride** in their country.

5. Our teacher handed us small U.N. **flags**.

6. The flag of the Olympic Games brings everyone a **message**.

7. The five rings show us five major **areas** of the world.

8. The blue ring gives Europe its **identification**.

9. The red ring brings Americans **respect**.

10. The interlocking circles give participants a positive **image**.

Write an indirect object for each sentence. You may use words and phrases from the Word Bank or choose your own. **Answers may vary. Possible responses appear below.**

## Word Bank

| | | | |
|---|---|---|---|
| citizens | competitors | wounded | nations |
| sister | world | athletes | us |
| band | people | Olympic Games | Olympic flag |
| participants | victims | me | everyone |
| member nations | | | |

11. The U.N. flag shows the _____ viewer _____ a view of the globe from the North Pole.

12. The 189 flags at the U.N. grant all _____ member nations _____ recognition.

13. The United Nations affords the _____ world _____ a hope for peace.

14. Artists gave the _____ Olympic flag _____ five interlocking rings to represent geographic areas around the world.

15. The interlocking rings on the Olympic flag give the _____ participants _____ a feeling of unity.

16. The Olympic Games grant over 11,000 _____ athletes _____ an opportunity to compete with other national representatives.

17. The 2000 Summer Games provided _____ competitors _____ the chance to represent 199 countries.

18. The Red Cross flag is another flag that offers _____ nations _____ encouragement.

19. Red Cross workers teach _____ us _____ lifesaving techniques.

20. The Red Cross provides _____ victims _____ of disaster great relief.

21. The parade marshal handed my _____ sister _____ the first flag.

22. She gave _____ me _____ the second one.

23. Then she sent the _____ band _____ a signal to begin to play.

# Predicate Nouns and Predicate Adjectives

## Learn

American Samoa became a United States **territory** in 1904.
Its flag is quite **attractive**.

Which boldfaced noun tells more about who or what the subject is? _____ territory _____

Which boldfaced adjective tells how the subject looks or feels? _____ attractive _____

> A **predicate noun** follows a linking verb and renames the subject.
> A **predicate adjective** follows a linking verb and describes the subject.

## Practice

Circle the linking verb in each sentence. Write **PN** for each boldfaced word that is a predicate noun. Write **PA** for each boldfaced word that is a predicate adjective.

1. The capital of the largest island in American Samoa (is) **Pago Pago**.          PN

2. The background of the American Samoa flag (is) **blue**.          PA

3. The people of Samoa (are) **proud** of their flag and their land.          PA

4. Another U.S. territory (is) **Guam**.          PN

5. The object in the center of the Guam flag (is) a palm **tree**.          PN

6. The U.S. Virgin Islands (are) **islands** in the Caribbean.          PN

7. The eagle on the flag (is) **yellow** and holds a U.S. shield.          PA

8. The letters *V I* (are) **part** of the design on the flag of the U.S. Virgin Islands.          PN

9. The terrain of the Virgin Islands (is) **rugged** and **hilly**.          PA

10. Puerto Rico (is) a **commonwealth** associated with the U.S.          PN

11. The capital of Puerto Rico (is) **San Juan**.          PN

12. The colors of the flag of Puerto Rico (are) **red**, **white**, and **blue**.          PA

# Apply

Write a predicate noun or a predicate adjective to complete each sentence. You may use the words from the Word Bank or choose your own words. (13.–27.)

## Word Bank

| | | | | | |
|---|---|---|---|---|---|
| stars | seat | D.C. | coat of arms | popular | hero |
| symbol | red | white | proud | interesting | monument |
| beautiful | true | familiar | important | different | wonderful |

The District of Columbia is the _____ seat _____ of the United States government. The abbreviation for the District of Columbia is _____ D.C. _____ . The Smithsonian buildings are _____ popular _____ with tourists and historians.

The District of Columbia has a flag. The basis of the flag's design is George Washington's _____ coat of arms _____ . The three figures on the top part of the flag are red _____ stars _____ . The two stripes below the stars are also _____ red _____ . The background is plain _____ white _____ . The arrangement of these stars and stripes is _____ different _____ from that of our national flag.

George Washington has been a _____ hero _____ to Americans for many years. His place in U.S. history is very _____ important _____ . His influence extends beyond his deeds. The flag of the District of Columbia is also a _____ symbol _____ of his importance. The Washington Monument is a _____ monument _____ in the heart of the city.

The U.S. flag is more _____ familiar _____ than the District of Columbia flag. That fact is _____ true _____ even for D.C. citizens. Nevertheless, they are _____ proud _____ of their red and white flag.

# Prepositional Phrases

## Learn

Abraham Lincoln took office in 1861.

Which words tell when Lincoln became president? _____in 1861_____

> A **prepositional phrase** can tell *how, what kind, when, how much,* or *where*. A prepositional phrase begins with a **preposition,** such as *in, over, of, to,* or *by*. It ends with a noun or pronoun that is the **object of the preposition**. Words between the preposition and the object of the preposition are also part of the prepositional phrase. A prepositional phrase can appear at the beginning, the middle, or the end of a sentence.

## Practice

Underline each prepositional phrase. Circle the preposition that begins the phrase. There may be more than one phrase in each sentence.

1. Southern states seceded (from) the Union.

2. Confederate soldiers soon fired (on) Fort Sumter.

3. Southern forces defeated the Union army (at) the battle (of) Bull Run.

4. The outnumbered Confederate soldiers rallied (around) Stonewall Jackson.

5. Union troops trained (in) the streets (of) Washington, D.C.

6. General Robert E. Lee was a graduate (of) West Point.

7. Union forces suffered several defeats (at) the hands (of) General Lee.

8. (In) 1863, Lee invaded the state (of) Pennsylvania.

9. Union General Meade pushed Lee's army (from) the state.

10. Lincoln promoted Ulysses Grant (to) the rank (of) lieutenant general.

Write each sentence, adding one of the prepositional phrases in the box.
Use a history book or encyclopedia if you need to.

## Word Bank

in January 1863                    on the Gettysburg battlefield
with Lee's surrender               after Lincoln's death
at Appomattox, Virginia            within a military fort
in New York City                   at Ford's Theatre

11. The Civil War ended in 1865.

The Civil War ended in 1865 with Lee's surrender.

12. Lincoln gave a famous address.

Lincoln gave a famous address on the Gettysburg battlefield.

13. Lincoln signed the Emancipation Proclamation.

Lincoln signed the Emancipation Proclamation in January 1863.

14. Lee signed the surrender.

Lee signed the surrender at Appomattox, Virginia.

15. Lincoln was assassinated.

Lincoln was assassinated at Ford's Theatre.

16. Andrew Johnson became president.

Andrew Johnson became president after Lincoln's death.

17. Jefferson Davis, the Confederate president, was imprisoned.

Jefferson Davis, the Confederate president, was imprisoned within a military fort.

18. Grant is buried.

Grant is buried in New York City.

# Compound Sentences

## Learn

a. Mexico consists of 31 states **and** the Federal District.
b. The president of Mexico serves six years in office, **but** a member of the Federal Chamber of Deputies serves three years.

Write the boldfaced conjunction in each sentence. _____and____but____

Which sentence, **a.** or **b.**, could become two separate sentences? ___b.___

> A **compound sentence** is made up of two or more closely related simple sentences. A simple sentence is also called an *independent clause*. In a compound sentence, the two clauses can be joined by a comma and a conjunction (*and, but, or*) or by a semicolon (;).

## Practice

Write **S** next to each simple sentence and **C** next to each compound sentence. Then underline the independent clauses in the compound sentences.

___C___ **1.** The president of Mexico appoints 17 Cabinet members, but the 31 governors are elected.

___S___ **2.** The two political parties are the Partido Revolucionario Institucional and the Partido de Acción Nacional.

___S___ **3.** The Aztecs controlled most of Mexico and established a capital in central Mexico.

___S___ **4.** The Spanish arrived in 1519 and found many highly developed civilizations.

___C___ **5.** Tribes in the North were hunters and gatherers; those in the South were farmers.

___C___ **6.** The Aztecs were Native Americans from northern Mexico, and they dominated northern Mexico at the time the Spanish arrived.

___C___ **7.** Many Aztecs were killed by the Spanish, or they died from diseases like measles.

___S___ **8.** They had no natural defense against European diseases and no medicines to cure them.

___S___ **9.** Mexico got its name from the Aztec war god Mexitli but continued to be a Spanish colony for over 200 years.

___S___ **10.** Mexico fought for its independence and gained it in the early 1800s.

Write compound sentences by combining the pairs of simple sentences. Circle the conjunction or semicolon you add. **Answers will vary. Possible responses appear below.**

11. For more than a half century, independent Mexico made little economic progress. The peasants suffered greatly.

   For more than a half century, independent Mexico made little economic progress,(and) the

   peasants suffered greatly.

12. Benito Juárez became president in 1858. He quickly seized all church property. _____

   Benito Juárez became president in 1858,(and) he quickly seized all church property.

13. Juárez wanted the peasants to get this property. The wealthy soon bought most of it.

   Juárez wanted the peasants to get this property,(but) the wealthy soon bought most of it.

14. The British, French, and Spanish landed at Veracruz. The French overthrew the Mexican government.

   The British, French, and Spanish landed at Veracruz,(and) the French overthrew

   the Mexican government.

15. The Mexican army won a big battle with the French on May 5, 1862. This victory is celebrated as Cinco de Mayo.

   The Mexican army won a big battle with the French on May 5, 1862(;) this victory

   is celebrated as Cinco de Mayo.

16. The U.S. demanded that the French leave Mexico. The U.S. would send troops if necessary.

   The U.S. demanded that the French leave Mexico,(or) the U.S. would send troops if necessary.

17. The French withdrew. The French emperor was executed. _____

   The French withdrew,(and) the French emperor was executed.

18. Years of turmoil followed. Porfirio Díaz finally emerged as president. _____

   Years of turmoil followed,(but) Porfirio Díaz finally emerged as president.

# Dependent and Independent Clauses

## Learn

When Churchill became prime minister, he faced many challenges.
<u>a.</u>          <u>b.</u>

Which clause, **a.** or **b.**, makes sense by itself? _____ b.

> An **independent clause** is a sentence and makes sense by itself. A **dependent clause** has a subject and a verb, but it does not make sense by itself. It needs—or is dependent on—an independent clause. A dependent clause often begins with a word such as *although, because, if, as,* or *when.*

## Practice

Underline each dependent clause. Circle the word that begins each dependent clause.

1. Winston Churchill was born (when) his father entered Parliament.

2. (As) Winston grew to maturity, his grandfather served as viceroy of Ireland.

3. (Because) his family spent time abroad, Winston attended private schools in England.

4. Churchill was not a promising student, (although) he excelled in English.

5. (When) he was 16, Churchill entered a historic British military college.

6. (Although) his assignment in the infantry kept him busy, Churchill always found time to read.

7. Churchill ran for a seat in Parliament in 1899 (when) he returned from India.

8. (Although) he lost the election, Churchill was not discouraged.

9. (Because) he had become a hero in the Boer War, Churchill's second run for office was successful.

10. (If) Churchill rose to speak, the other members of Parliament listened attentively.

Add an independent clause to either the beginning or the end of each dependent clause. Write the complete sentence. **Answers will vary.**

11. because Churchill possessed great speaking ability _____

_____

12. although his grades were poor _____

_____

13. if Churchill had a spare moment _____

_____

14. as Churchhill grew up _____

_____

15. when he went to war _____

_____

16. even though his parents traveled often _____

_____

17. by the time he was 12 years old _____

_____

18. after he lost the election _____

_____

19. whenever Churchill could find time _____

_____

20. when the Boer War ended _____

_____

# Avoiding Fragments, Run-ons, Comma Splices

## Learn

___S___ Churchill painted under a different name.

___RO___ He won a Nobel prize for literature his writing earned him money.

___F___ gradually slipped from view.

___CS___ Churchill warned the world about Germany, his warnings were ignored.

Write **S** by the correct sentence. Write **RO** by the sentence that needs a comma and a conjunction. Write **F** by the sentence that is not a complete thought. Write **CS** by the sentence that has a comma but needs a conjunction.

> A **fragment** does not tell a complete thought. A **run-on sentence** is two sentences that are run together without a comma and a conjunction. A **comma splice** is two sentences that are joined only by a comma but are missing a conjunction.

## Practice

Write **F** by each sentence fragment. Write **RO** by each run-on sentence. Write **CS** by each sentence that has a comma splice. Write **S** by each complete sentence.

___RO___ **1.** Prime Minister Chamberlain was forced to resign Churchill succeeded him.

___S___ **2.** Churchill addressed the British people, but he said he offered only "blood, toil, tears, and sweat."

___CS___ **3.** Churchill feared the Communist threat, he nevertheless worked with Soviet Premier Stalin.

___S___ **4.** Churchill's party lost the election in 1945, and Churchill was forced to resign as prime minister.

___RO___ **5.** Churchill never lost his powerful speaking ability one of his best-known speeches was given in Fulton, Missouri.

___F___ **6.** Coined the term "Iron Curtain."

Rewrite each of these fragments, run-on sentences, and comma splices correctly. **Answers will vary.**

7. rose to prominence during World War II

_____

_____

8. Britain and the Soviet Union declared war on Germany, after Pearl Harbor the United States also joined the war.

_____

_____

9. The Cold War began in 1946 it lasted until 1989.

_____

_____

10. The Cold War refers to a time of tension, war was never declared.

_____

_____

11. Setbacks rarely discouraged Churchill he always seemed to bounce back.

_____

_____

12. Churchill possessed many talents, none were more important than his leadership in a crisis.

_____

_____

13. Churchill called Nazi Germany a monstrous tyranny, he vowed to defeat it.

_____

_____

14. formed a "V for Victory." _____

_____

# Common and Proper Nouns

## Learn

Our **planet,** (**Earth**) is a small planet in the **universe** when compared to (**Jupiter**)

Underline the boldfaced nouns that name any place.
Circle the boldfaced nouns that name a particular place.

> A **common noun** names any person, place, thing, or idea. A **proper noun** names a particular person, place, thing, or idea. Proper nouns must be capitalized.

## Practice

Circle the common nouns. Underline the proper nouns.

1. A (solar system) is made up of a (star) and any (objects) that travel around that (star)

2. The largest (planet) in our solar (system) is Jupiter, which is 88,700 (miles) in (diameter)

3. Jupiter is more than 11 (times) larger than Earth.

4. Jupiter was named for the (king) of the (gods) according to the (mythology) of the Romans.

5. The four largest (bodies) that revolve around Jupiter are Ganymede, Io, Europa, and Callisto.

6. The (moons) of Jupiter are named for mythological (figures) of ancient Greece.

7. The (moon) that revolves around Earth does not have a special (name.)

8. The (planet) Saturn is also much larger than Earth.

9. Its (name) comes from the (god) the Romans said was responsible for (agriculture)

10. Four (planets)—Mercury, Venus, Earth, and Mars—are closer to the (sun) than Jupiter is.

11. Saturn stands out from other (planets) because of its (rings)

12. (Billions) of (pieces) of (ice) make up the seven (rings) that surround Saturn.

Rewrite these sentences correctly by capitalizing the proper nouns.

**13.** The planet mars has been the subject of many stories.

The planet Mars has been the subject of many stories.

**14.** Scientists want to know whether there might ever have been life on mars.

Scientists want to know whether there might ever have been life on Mars.

**15.** According to mythology, mars was the father of romulus, the founder of rome.

According to mythology, Mars was the father of Romulus, the founder of Rome.

**16.** In december of 1996, the united states sent a probe called pathfinder to mars.

In December of 1996, the United States sent a probe called Pathfinder to Mars.

**17.** On pathfinder was a robot named sojourner.

On Pathfinder was a robot named Sojourner.

**18.** Sojourner gathered information that went to pathfinder and back to earth.

Sojourner gathered information that went to Pathfinder and back to Earth.

**19.** Venus is most like earth in size, mass, and density.

Venus is most like Earth in size, mass, and density.

**20.** The planet venus is only about 400 miles smaller than earth.

The planet Venus is only about 400 miles smaller than Earth.

# Plural and Possessive Nouns

## Learn

The construction of the **astronauts' suits** allows the **astronauts** to breathe outside **Earth's** atmosphere.

Circle the parts of the words *astronauts'* and *Earth's* that show possession.
Underline the parts of the words *suits* and *astronauts* that show they mean more than one person or thing.

> A **plural noun** names more than one person, place, thing, or idea. Most nouns add -*s* to form the plural. Some nouns change spelling instead of adding -*s* (*woman/women*). Some nouns have the same singular and plural form (*deer*). A **possessive noun** shows ownership. Most plural nouns add an apostrophe after the *s* to form the possessive (*boys'*). Plurals that don't end in -*s*, such as *children*, add apostrophe and -*s* to show possession (*children's*).

## Practice

Underline each plural noun. Circle each possessive noun. Then write each noun that is both plural and possessive. Not every sentence has a plural possessive noun.

1. Space has always stirred scientists' interests and imaginations.

   _____ scientists'

2. Humans have actually visited places beyond Earth.

   _____

3. At first, the spacecrafts did not have humans aboard.

   _____

4. The first spacecraft was the former Soviet Union's satellite *Sputnik*.

   _____

5. We call that date the space age's beginning.

   _____

6. The Soviets' spaceship showed that a person could be sent into space.

   _____ Soviets'

7. The *Apollo 8* spacecraft's voyage in 1968 was the first of the orbits around the moon by humans.

   _____

Write a plural noun (**Pl**), possessive noun (**Poss**), or plural possessive noun (**Pl Poss**) to replace the boldfaced singular nouns.

8. When **people** (**Pl Poss**) _____ people's _____ interest in space travel began, they had to figure out how to live in space.

9. Without **Earth** (**Poss**) _____ Earth's _____ air, **astronaut** (**Pl**) _____ astronauts _____ wouldn't be able to breathe.

10. Much less gravity in space would also make living **condition** (**Pl**) _____ conditions _____ difficult.

11. In a spacecraft, fuel must be squeezed out of the fuel **tank** (**Pl**) _____ tanks _____ .

12. **Astronaut** (**Pl Poss**) _____ Astronauts' _____ **situation** (**Pl**) _____ situations _____ had to be studied carefully by **scientist** (**Pl**) _____ scientists _____ .

13. Many space **traveler** (**Pl**) _____ travelers _____ get sick during the first few **day** (**Pl Poss**) _____ days' _____ travel.

14. **Traveler** (**Pl**) _____ Travelers _____ in space **vehicle** (**Pl**) _____ vehicles _____ also must exercise vigorously to keep their heart **muscle** (**Pl**) _____ muscles _____ strong.

15. Scientific **plan** (**Pl**) _____ plans _____ for **astronaut** (**Pl Poss**) _____ astronauts' _____ basic **need** (**Pl**) _____ needs _____ have been quite creative.

16. Now it is possible to heat frozen **meal** (**Pl**) _____ meals _____ on board.

17. There are special **fan** (**Pl**) _____ fans _____ for circulating the **spacecraft** (**Poss**) _____ spacecraft's _____ air.

18. Special **device** (**Pl**) _____ devices _____ produce safe water.

19. Sleeping is possible in sleeping **bag** (**Pl**) _____ bags _____ with **strap** (**Pl**) _____ straps _____ to hold the **sleeper** (**Pl**) _____ sleepers _____ in place.

20. Many of human **being** (**Pl Poss**) _____ beings' _____ **dream** (**Pl**) _____ dreams _____ of space travel have come true.

# Personal and Possessive Pronouns

## Learn

Modern scientists are not the first to study the sun, the moon, and the stars. Ancient people thought about **them,** too, but **their** calculations were not very accurate.

Which boldfaced word refers to the sun, moon, and stars? _____them_____

Which boldfaced word refers to ancient people? _____their_____

A **pronoun** can take the place of a noun. Use the **personal pronouns** *I, me, we,* and *us* to speak or write about yourself. Use the personal pronouns *you, he, him, she, her, it, they,* and *them* to refer to other people and things. The **possessive pronouns** *my, your, his, her, its, our,* and *their* show ownership.

## Practice

Underline each personal pronoun. Circle each possessive pronoun.

1. In ancient times, people thought (their) own living area was all there was to the universe.

2. They thought of the sun and moon as (their) gods.

3. Around 434 B.C., a Greek philosopher figured that the sun was 35 miles in diameter.

4. Scientists now estimate (its) diameter to be about 865,000 miles.

5. With the invention of the telescope, we have found out many details about the universe.

6. Scientists study the distance of a faraway object by (its) brightness.

7. Some astronomers and mathematicians think they have evidence that the universe is expanding.

8. We expect them to explain (their) new theories.

9. The universe is always in motion, but we do not know how some bodies in space are moving.

10. Scientists would not have been able to plan moon landings, though, if they hadn't figured out how fast Earth and the moon move.

Write one or more pronouns to complete each sentence. Use pronouns from the Word Bank. Use capital letters where they are needed.

## Word Bank

| it | we | she | he | him | her | I | they | me |
|---|---|---|---|---|---|---|---|---|
| them | their | our | its | his | your | my | you | us |

11. Earth revolves once around _____**its**_____ sun every 365 days.

12. _____**We**_____ call this revolution _____**our**_____ year.

13. When an astronomer makes a new discovery, _____**he or she**_____ compares it with what previous astronomers have known.

14. The Greek astronomer Ptolemy thought _____**he**_____ had figured out that the sun and the moon moved around Earth.

15. _____**His**_____ mistake was based on what _____**he**_____ could observe without the aid of a telescope.

16. About 1,400 years later, in 1543, Copernicus used _____**his**_____ reasoning ability to decide that all the planets revolve around the sun.

17. Most people did not believe _____**him**_____ , though.

18. Today there are space stations that keep _____**their**_____ passengers in space for extended periods of time.

19. On March 25, 2001, the astronauts on board the International Space Station gave _____**their**_____ viewers on Earth an unusual treat.

20. _____**They**_____ appeared at the beginning of the Academy Awards ceremony.

21. U.S. astronaut Susan Helms spoke to _____**their/her**_____ television audience.

22. _____**She**_____ and _____**her**_____ crewmates floated inside their spacecraft in front of millions of viewers.

23. The space program made _____**its**_____ first Hollywood appearance.

# The Present Tense

## Learn

Light **travels** at a speed of 186,282 miles per second.
The physicist Albert Michelson **discovered** this fact in 1926.

Underline the boldfaced word that tells you something is happening right now or is true now.

> The **present tense** of a verb indicates that something happens regularly or is true now. When the subject is *he, she, it,* or a singular noun, form the present tense of most verbs by adding -*s* to the verb. Add -*es* to verbs ending in *s, ch, sh, x,* or *z*. Drop the *y* and add -*ies* to verbs ending in a consonant and *y*. Most verbs that follow plural nouns do not end in *s*.

## Practice

Underline the present-tense verb or verbs in each sentence.

1. Like sound and the family car, light moves at a certain speed.

2. When you flip a switch, light flies across the room almost immediately.

3. Light from the sun travels 90 million miles before reaching Earth.

4. The trip to Earth takes more than eight minutes.

5. The moon gets its light from the sun.

6. The sun's light reflects off the moon.

7. Two seconds later, moonlight reaches Earth.

8. Like the sun, stars produce their own light.

9. Light from some distant stars requires years before reaching Earth.

10. Scientists measure distance in light-years.

11. A light-year represents the distance light travels in a year.

12. Light speeds along at 5,870 billion miles in a year.

*Strategies for Writers*—Conventions & Skills Practice   Unit 2

Write the present-tense verb in parentheses to complete each sentence.

13. Light _____**comes**_____ (comes, came) to Earth from Alpha Centauri, our nearest star.

14. Alpha Centauri's light _____**passes**_____ (passed, passes) through space for over four years before reaching us.

15. That _____**means**_____ (meant, means) that light left Alpha Centauri over four years ago.

16. No one knows what _____**happens**_____ (happens, happened) on Alpha Centauri when it occurs.

17. We only _____**see**_____ (see, saw) evidence of what happened many years ago.

18. The planet Jupiter _____**travels**_____ (travels, traveled) in an elliptical orbit around the sun.

19. It _____**stays**_____ (stays, stayed) between 391 million miles and 600 million miles from Earth.

20. So the light reflected by Jupiter _____**takes**_____ (takes, took) between 35 minutes and 53 minutes to get to us.

21. Probably not much new _____**happens**_____ (happens, happened) on Jupiter while we _____**wait**_____ (wait, waits) for its light.

22. We usually _____**think**_____ (think, thought) we _____**see**_____ (see, saw) things as they happen.

23. Scientists _____**study**_____ (study, studied) the stars and how they _____**change**_____ (change, changed) with the passing of time.

24. They _____**use**_____ (use, used) information they _____**gather**_____ (gather, gathered) from telescopes all over the world.

25. Research _____**continues**_____ (continues, continued) as long as information about space is available.

# The Past and Future Tenses

## Learn

a. Scientists **predicted** a total eclipse of the sun.
b. We **will view** the eclipse from my porch.

Which sentence, **a.** or **b.,** has a verb that tells of an event that has already happened? ___a.___

Which sentence has a verb phrase that tells of something that will happen in the future? ___b.___

> A **past-tense verb** tells about something that has already happened. Regular verbs form the past tense by adding -*ed*. Irregular verbs change their spelling in the past tense. A **future-tense verb** tells what is going to happen in the future. Use the helping verb *will* with the verb to form the future tense.

## Practice

Underline each verb that is in the past tense. Circle each verb that is in the future tense.

1. Long ago, people thought the sun moved around Earth.

2. To them, the sun came up in the east and disappeared in the west.

3. Moreover, the sun seemed much smaller than our own planet.

4. In time, scientists discovered the truth about the sun's size.

5. We will know more about the sun as a result of the space program.

6. Perhaps scientists will learn more about the sun's origins.

7. At some point, our solar system became part of the Milky Way galaxy.

8. Telescopes in space will reveal new information about the universe.

9. What forces formed our disk-shaped galaxy, the Milky Way?

10. Perhaps someday people will travel outside our solar system and into the larger galaxy.

Rewrite each sentence. Change the present-tense verb in parentheses to either a past-tense verb or a future-tense verb to complete the sentence correctly. You will need to add *will* for the future tense.

**11.** Some time ago, scientists (discover) the size of the Milky Way. _____

    Some time ago, scientists discovered the size of the Milky Way.

**12.** They (find) it to be about 100,000 light-years wide. _____

    They found it to be about 100,000 light-years wide.

**13.** Clouds of dust (block) the view of scientists for many years. _____

    Clouds of dust (blocked/will block) the view of scientists for many years.

**14.** No one (travel) across the galaxy in the near future. _____

    No one will travel across the galaxy in the near future.

**15.** Scientists (compare) our sun to other stars in the Milky Way. _____

    Scientists compared our sun to other stars in the Milky Way.

**16.** They (conclude) that the sun is just average in size. _____

    They concluded that the sun is just average in size.

**17.** Studies also (reveal) information about the movement of the Milky Way.

    Studies also revealed information about the movement of the Milky Way.

**18.** It (appear) that stars (rotate) around the hub of the Milky Way. _____

    It appeared that stars rotated around the hub of the Milky Way.

**19.** Astronomers (say) that the sun and its planets take 250 million years for one round trip.

    Astronomers said that the sun and its planets take 250 million years for one round trip.

**20.** Astronomers (count) 17 galaxies within 2.5 million light-years of the Milky Way.

    Astronomers counted 17 galaxies within 2.5 million light-years of the Milky Way.

# The Present Perfect Tense

## Learn

The giant panda (has become) an endangered animal. Visitors to the zoos that house pandas **enjoy** seeing these rare animals.

Circle the boldfaced verb that tells about an action that began in the past and continues today.

> The **present perfect tense** indicates action that happened in the past and may be continuing. To form the present perfect tense, add the helping verb *has* or *have* to the past participle of a verb. The **past participle** of regular verbs is formed by adding *-ed* (*work/have worked*). Irregular verbs change their spelling to form past participles (*build/have built*).

## Practice

Underline the ten verbs below that are in the present perfect tense. Be sure to include the helping verbs. **(1.–10.)**

Zoologists have shown that there are two kinds of pandas. However, some zoologists have disagreed about how to classify the two pandas. One group of scientists has labeled them the giant panda and the red panda. Both varieties pick up their food with their paws the way raccoons do. This behavior has entertained many zoo visitors. Scientists noticed that the red panda's tail is similar to that of the raccoon. This fact has led scientists to group the red panda in the same family as the raccoon. However, the giant panda has puzzled scientists. Some have thought the giant panda also to be part of the raccoon family. Others call the giant panda a "panda bear." Today, most zoologists classify the giant panda as a bear.

Few pandas have survived in the wild. Those that still exist are found in China. The Chinese have taken steps to protect this rare animal. So far, their efforts have stopped further loss of this beautiful animal.

Write the present perfect form (*has* or *have* plus the past participle) of the verb in parentheses to complete each sentence.

**11.** The number of giant pandas in the world __has decreased__ dramatically. (decrease)

**12.** One reason is that much of their food supply __has died__ . (die)

**13.** Bamboo __has provided__ the major source of food for the panda. (provide)

**14.** Several types of bamboo __have grown__ successfully in several parts of the world. (grow)

**15.** In some places it __has reached__ as high as 120 feet. (reach)

**16.** Giant pandas __have preferred__ eating only a few types of bamboo. (prefer)

**17.** Because they produce seeds only every 30 to 100 years, some species of bamboo __have disappeared__ . (disappear)

**18.** Therefore, the number of pandas __has declined__ . (decline)

**19.** Some people __have tried__ planting bamboo in new areas. (try)

**20.** Even those plants __have bloomed__ only after years of waiting. (bloom)

**21.** The government of China __has loaned__ giant pandas to zoos in the United States. (loan)

**22.** This __has meant__ that many people can appreciate seeing these beautiful animals. (mean)

**23.** Zoos also __have tried__ to breed giant pandas but without much success. (try)

**24.** People __have agreed__ that the best thing for giant pandas would be for them to continue to exist in the wild. (agree)

**25.** No matter how scientists __have classified__ them, everyone will love their cute faces and fluffy bodies. (classify)

# Adjectives

## Learn

The U.S. Fish & Wildlife Service keeps a list of (threatened) and (endangered) animals.

Circle two words that describe the animals on the list.

> **Adjectives** describe nouns and pronouns. Some adjectives tell **what kind**. Others, like *many* and *six*, tell **how many**. The adjectives *this, that, these,* and *those* tell **which one**. These are called *demonstrative adjectives*. The articles *a, an,* and *the* are also adjectives.

## Practice

Write **what kind, how many,** or **which one** to tell what the boldfaced adjective tells about the noun.

1. There are **63** species of mammals on the list of endangered animals. _____how many_____

2. Others are considered **threatened** animals. _____what kind_____

3. Worldwide, the list has an even **higher** number. _____what kind_____

4. There are few plans to save **these** species. _____which one_____

5. **Large** mammals are not the only threatened species. _____what kind_____

6. The list includes colorful birds and **tiny** turtles. _____what kind_____

7. An endangered species has so **few** living members that it might disappear altogether. _____how many_____

8. The bald eagle, our **national** symbol, was once a rarity. _____what kind_____

9. After years of **careful** protection, the number of eagles began to increase. _____what kind_____

10. The survival of the eagle was cause for **great** celebration. _____what kind_____

11. The **Aleutian** Canada goose has also avoided extinction. _____what kind_____

12. **This** bird was taken off the list in 2001. _____which one_____

**Apply**

Select an adjective from the Word Bank to complete each sentence. The adjective should give the information shown in parentheses. You may use a word more than once, and not every word will be used. **Answers may vary. Possible responses appear below.**

## Word Bank

| whooping | long | several | endangered | beautiful |
| tallest | usual | threatened | many | old |
| these | shallow | numerous | familiar | up-to-date |

13. The whooping crane is the _____tallest_____ American bird. (what kind)

14. Whooping cranes have _____long_____ necks and legs. (what kind)

15. _____These_____ birds have snow-white feathers with black wing tips. (which ones)

16. There are many _____beautiful_____ species of birds on our continent. (what kind)

17. Whooping cranes have been on the _____endangered_____ species list for many years. (what kind)

18. Over the last _____several_____ years, however, the whooping cranes have been recovering. (how many)

19. _____These_____ cranes were dying out because their homes were being destroyed. (which ones)

20. The _____usual_____ habitats of whooping cranes are wetlands and grasslands. (what kind)

21. In the wetlands, the cranes sleep standing up in _____shallow_____ water. (what kind)

22. Now _____many_____ efforts have been made to save the whooping cranes. (how many)

23. Each year, some of these birds have been reintroduced into their _____old_____ habitat. (what kind)

24. The U.S. Fish & Wildlife Service asks for _____up-to-date_____ reports from anyone seeing these birds during their migration periods. (what kind)

# Adverbs

## Learn

Alligators **usually** move **slowly**. An alligator's jaw and tail are **very** strong.

Which boldfaced word tells how alligators move? _____slowly_____

Which boldfaced word tells when alligators move? _____usually_____

Which boldfaced word describes an adjective? _____very_____

> **Adverbs** describe verbs or adjectives. They tell **how, when, where,** or **to what extent** (how much). Many adverbs end in -*ly*. Other common adverbs are *fast, very, often, again, sometimes, soon, only, however, too, later, first, then, far,* and *now*.

## Practice

Underline each adverb in the sentences below.

1. Alligators live comfortably in the warm waters of southeastern United States.

2. The American alligator has a large, slightly rounded body.

3. Their short, rather thick legs are not suited to swimming.

4. Their powerful tails allow them to glide gracefully through water.

5. As a result, alligators can move quickly and quietly.

6. These reptiles have sharply pointed teeth and very strong jaws.

7. Alligators eat primarily fish, turtles, and snails.

8. In the past, hunters often killed alligators for their valuable skin.

9. The loss of many wetlands nearly caused alligators to disappear.

10. The government then decided to place the American alligator on the endangered species list.

Add an adverb to describe the boldfaced word in each sentence. You may use words from the Word Bank if you wish. **Answers will vary. Possible responses appear below.**

## Word Bank

| | | | |
|---|---|---|---|
| easily | closely | more | high |
| greatly | viciously | definitely | tightly |
| clearly | constantly | brightly | carefully |

11. If an alligator **closes** its jaws _____tightly_____ , it is difficult to open them.

12. Alligators and crocodiles are alike in many ways but **differ** _____greatly_____ in other ways.

13. If you **look** _____closely_____ at a crocodile's mouth, you will notice something interesting.

14. The crocodile's fourth tooth can be _____clearly_____ **seen**.

15. If you see this tooth, you are _____actually_____ **looking** at a crocodile, not an alligator.

16. The alligator moves _____more_____ **slowly** than a crocodile because it is heavier.

17. Crocodiles have been known to **attack** large animals and humans _____viciously_____ .

18. The eyes of both alligators and crocodiles are **placed** _____high_____ on their heads.

19. They **watch** _____constantly_____ for prey while their bodies are hidden in the water.

20. A crocodile can _____easily_____ **live** to be 60 years old.

21. Crocodile moms sometimes help their babies hatch by _____carefully_____ cracking the eggs.

22. Alligator babies have _____brightly_____ colored stripes and patches, which disappear as they get older.

# Prepositions

## Learn

The life spans **of** animals can vary widely. Some turtles and tortoises live **over** 100 years.

Which boldfaced word begins a phrase that tells about a noun? _____ *of* _____

Which two nouns does this boldfaced word link? _____ *spans, animals* _____

Which boldfaced word begins a phrase that tells *how long*? _____ *over* _____

> A **preposition** shows a relationship between one word in a sentence and the noun or pronoun that follows the preposition. The noun or pronoun that follows the preposition is the **object of the preposition**. The preposition, the object of the preposition, and the words between them make a **prepositional phrase**.

## Practice

Underline the prepositional phrase in each sentence. Draw a second line under the preposition. Circle the object of the preposition. Some sentences have more than one prepositional phrase.

1. Some of the world's animals live longer than humans do.

2. The common box tortoise can live for 130 years.

3. A tortoise called Marion's tortoise has lived over 150 years.

4. Once in a while we hear that a human has lived 100 years.

5. Humans and fin whales have the longest life spans of any mammals.

6. Some animals' life spans have increased when they are in captivity.

7. Others live longer when left in the wild.

8. Animals with many natural enemies are protected in a zoo.

9. Zoos also provide medical care for their animals.

10. Many animals in their natural habitat die from disease.

# Apply

Complete each sentence with an appropriate preposition from the Word Bank. You may use words more than once. If the preposition comes at the beginning of a sentence, be sure to capitalize it.

## Word Bank

| with | between | about | on | of | in | without |
|------|---------|-------|-----|-----|------|---------|
| inside | around | to | for | near | within | |

11. Household pets live much longer when they are kept _____ in _____ the house.

12. An indoor cat's average life span is _____ about _____ 18 years.

13. The average length _____ of _____ an outdoor cat's life is two years.

14. There are many dangers _____ for _____ a cat who goes outside.

15. Car accidents are the most common cause _____ of _____ death.

16. Outdoor cats are dangerous _____ to _____ other animals, too.

17. The record age _____ of _____ a domestic cat is 34 years.

18. Either the cat was very lucky or it stayed _____ inside _____ the house.

19. The oldest chimpanzee _____ on _____ record is 50 years old.

20. Human life expectancy _____ in _____ the United States is _____ between _____ 76 and 78 years.

21. Longer life spans are becoming more common _____ with _____ better health care.

22. It is thought, though, that humans could live _____ around _____ 150 years.

23. _____ With _____ the proper diet and exercise, a person can live a long time.

24. _____ Without _____ medicine, people lived much shorter lives.

25. Not long ago, people were expected to live only _____ about _____ fifty years.

# Coordinating and Subordinating Conjunctions

## Learn

Life on Earth continues in part **because** the water cycle provides nutrients **and** other necessities of life.

Which boldfaced word links the things water provides? _____ and _____

Which boldfaced word links the second part of the sentence to the first part

of the sentence? _____ because _____

> **Coordinating conjunctions** (*and, but, or*) connect words or groups of words (including independent clauses) of equal importance. **Subordinating conjunctions,** such as *although, because, as, so, if,* and *before,* relate one clause to another clause and signal that the clause that follows is "dependent" on an independent clause.

## Practice

Circle each coordinating conjunction. Underline each subordinating conjunction.

1. Water is essential to us because our bodies are about two-thirds water.

2. Plants, animals, and people must have water.

3. Although water evaporates, it is recycled and returns to the earth.

4. The water cycle refers to the circulation of moisture as it changes form.

5. Rain seeps into the ground and makes its way into the water table.

6. Rain also fills lakes, rivers, and oceans.

7. We purify the water and use it for drinking.

8. Moisture rises from the ground and from bodies of water because the sun's heat evaporates it.

9. Although we use much water, great amounts are left to evaporate.

10. The vapor forms water again in the air, and rain falls.

Combine a sentence part from Column 1 with a sentence part from Column 2 to write a sentence. Circle the coordinating conjunctions and underline the subordinating conjunctions.

**Column 1**
The clouds contain snow

Some rain falls on mountains

Rivers provide us with water

Water vapor forms clouds

Most of the rain falls on the oceans

Water falls as rain or snow

All the water that ever was still exists

**Column 2**
where gravity pulls it down to rivers and lakes.

if the air is chilled enough.

when there is no rain.

because oceans cover about 70 percent of the earth.

after it has condensed.

before the rain falls.

because the water cycle keeps it moving in different forms.

11. The clouds contain snow <u>if</u> the air is chilled enough.

12. Some rain falls on mountains, <u>where</u> gravity pulls it down to rivers (and) lakes.

13. Rivers provide us with water <u>when</u> there is no rain.

14. Water vapor forms clouds <u>before</u> the rain falls.

15. Most of the rain falls on the oceans <u>because</u> oceans cover about 70 percent of the earth.

16. Water falls as rain (or) snow <u>after</u> it has condensed.

17. All the water that ever was still exists <u>because</u> the water cycle keeps it moving in different forms.

# Their, There, They're

## Learn

After the 2000 census, the people of Edgar Springs, Missouri, learned that **they're** famous for something. The population hub of the United States is right **there** in **their** small town.

Which boldfaced word is a contraction of the words *they* and *are*? _____they're_____

Which boldfaced word means "belonging to them"? _____their_____

Which boldfaced word refers to a place? _____there_____

> The words **their, there,** and **they're** sound alike, but they have different spellings and meanings. *Their* is a possessive pronoun meaning "belonging to them." *There* is an adverb that means "in that place." *They're* is the contraction made from the words *they are.*

## Practice

Write the word in parentheses that correctly completes each sentence.

1. Would you like to go (their/there/they're) to be where the same number of people live in all directions?  _____there_____

2. Workers at the United States Census Bureau carry out (their/there/they're) task of counting the population every ten years.  _____their_____

3. In 1790, Americans learned that the center of (their/there/they're) young nation was near Baltimore, Maryland.  _____their_____

4. The population, however, would not remain (their/there/they're) very long.  _____there_____

5. Experts say (their/there/they're) certain that the population has now grown to 283 million.  _____they're_____

6. If you go (their/there/they're), the 190 people of Edgar Springs, Missouri, may want to brag about their new title.  _____there_____

7. (Their/There/They're) truly in the heartland of the nation.  _____They're_____

Write an answer to each question. Use **their, there,** or **they're** correctly in your answer. Remember to capitalize the first word of a sentence. **Answers will vary.**

8. Have you been to Edgar Springs, Missouri? _____

_____

9. How often are the people of the United States counted? _____

_____

10. Have you read the report of the Census Bureau? _____

_____

11. In which direction are the people of the United States moving? _____

_____

12. Why do you think people are moving to those areas? _____

_____

13. What do the people in the Census Bureau say the current population of the United States is?

_____

_____

14. Why did so many people live in the East in 1790? _____

_____

15. How do you think the people of Edgar Springs feel about being the population center of the United States?

_____

_____

# *Its* and *It's*

## Learn

In spite of years of study, Chaco Canyon refuses to give up **its** secrets. Archaeologists agree **it's** one of the great mysteries of the past.

Which boldfaced word means "belonging to Chaco Canyon"? ___its___

Which boldfaced word is a contraction made from the words *it* and *is*? ___it's___

> The words **its** and **it's** sound the same, but they have different spellings and meanings. *Its* is a possessive pronoun that means "belonging to it." *It's* is the contraction made from *it is* or *it has*.

## Practice

Circle the word in parentheses that correctly completes each sentence. (**1.–12.**)

Chaco Canyon, a site in northwestern New Mexico, is known for (it's/**its**) ancient ruins. (**It's**/Its) attracted tourists and scientists alike. Here in Chaco Canyon lie the ruins of an entire community of small villages that (**it's**/its) believed are at least 1,400 years old. The people who once lived in these villages were part of a group now called the Anasazi.

One of the villages in this canyon is called Pueblo Bonito. (It's/**Its**) name means "the pretty village," and (**it's**/its) the largest of all the villages. (**It's**/Its) probably over 1,000 years old. The shape of (it's/**its**) construction looks something like a large letter D. Pueblo Bonito probably had four or five stories in (it's/**its**) main dwelling. What can be seen now, however, are only (it's/**its**) lower floors and kivas. The kivas are round underground rooms where the community held (it's/**its**) religious ceremonies.

As in the other villages of Chaco Canyon, there is an open area, a plaza or courtyard. Scientists think the village held (it's/**its**) dances there. (**It's**/Its) also where day-to-day activities such as grinding corn and firing pottery probably took place.

Rewrite each sentence replacing the boldfaced words or phrases with words or phrases using **its** or **it's**. Remember to capitalize a word if it begins a sentence.

**13.** Pieces of pottery and jewelry found in Chaco Canyon tell us about **the early inhabitants**.

Pieces of pottery and jewelry found in Chaco Canyon tell us about its inhabitants.

**14.** **It is** interesting to study these items, called artifacts. _____

It's interesting to study these items, called artifacts.

**15.** Scientists who study a place and **the artifacts and ruins belonging to it** are called archaeologists.

Scientists who study a place and its artifacts and ruins are called archaeologists.

**16.** According to archaeologists, **it is** probable that the Anasazi wove distinctive baskets.

According to archaeologists, it's probable that the Anasazi wove distinctive baskets.

**17.** They found a scraping tool made of bone, and **the center belonging to it** had beautiful turquoise set into it.

They found a scraping tool made of bone, and its center had beautiful turquoise set into it.

**18.** From the discovery of turquoise jewelry, **it has** been assumed the Anasazi traded with other cultures.

From the discovery of turquoise jewelry, it's been assumed the Anasazi traded with other cultures.

**19.** Most of the jewelry in Chaco Canyon was found in Pueblo Bonito, the largest of **the villages belonging to it**.

Most of the jewelry in Chaco Canyon was found in Pueblo Bonito, the largest of its villages.

# *Your* and *You're*

## Learn

If **you're** interested in Native American culture, you will enjoy studying the Anasazi. **Your** research might include a visit to Arizona or New Mexico.

Which boldfaced word means "belonging to you"? ___*your*___

Which boldfaced word is a short form of *you are*? ___*you're*___

> The words **your** and **you're** sound the same, but they have different spellings and meanings. *Your* is a possessive pronoun. It means "belonging to you." *You're* is the contraction of the pronoun *you* and the verb *are*.

## Practice

Circle the word in parentheses that correctly completes each sentence in the conversation. (**1.–10.**)

"I hear (you're/your) doing a report on the Anasazi," Dylan said to Tonya. "What are (you're/your) findings so far?"

Tonya replied, "(You're/Your) going to be surprised at all I've learned. Did you know that the Anasazi go back 2,000 years?"

"(You're/Your) kidding, aren't you? How did you find out?" asked Dylan.

"I've been using (you're/your) book about early Americans," Tonya said with a smile. "(You're/Your) book has it all."

"(You're/Your) making me blush," admitted Dylan. Then he said, "If (you're/your) so smart, tell me what *Anasazi* means."

"That's easy. *Anasazi* is a word the Navajo use to mean ancestors, or the Ancient Ones. That's from (you're/your) own book. If you read the book, (you're/your) going to learn lots of interesting things about the Anasazi."

Draw a circle around every incorrect **your** and **you're**. You should find 14 errors. Then write the correct **your** or **you're** in order on each numbered line.

Dear Josie,

I was excited to read about you're trip to the Grand Canyon. Your seeing one of the most beautiful places on Earth. I was surprised to hear that so many of the walls seemed red in color. I hope your eyes weren't playing tricks on you.

Your never going to forget that hike you took down the trans-canyon trail. It must have been the highlight of you're entire trip. You're postcard said that your planning to take a river raft through the canyon next week. That sounds like great fun, but I hope your not in any danger.

I remember your cousin telling about taking a helicopter ride there. Is that part of you're plans? I know you're not too happy about plane rides, but I also know your brave enough to try it. (Just don't close you're eyes during the flight!)

Does your trip include a visit to Lake Mead? Your sure to enjoy it if you go there, but don't try to see everything on one trip. Your better off taking your time and enjoying yourself.

I can't wait for you're return. I hope your taking lots of pictures to show me.

Your friend,
Lynn

11. _____your_____    18. _____your_____

12. _____You're_____    19. _____you're_____

13. _____You're_____    20. _____your_____

14. _____your_____    21. _____You're_____

15. _____Your_____    22. _____You're_____

16. _____you're_____    23. _____your_____

17. _____you're_____    24. _____you're_____

# *Like* and *You Know*

## Learn

When we were, **like,** going on vacation, we wanted to see Chaco Canyon. It's, **you know,** a really interesting place. We **like** to see old ruins. Our teacher said that the more **you know** about your ancestors, the more **you know** about yourself.

Look at the boldfaced words above. Cross out the boldfaced words that interrupt the flow of communication.

> Some people develop the habit of using **like** or **you know** in places where they don't belong. This habit is annoying to most listeners and readers, and it certainly does not help communicate ideas clearly. Unless you are using *like* or *you know* as a meaningful part of a sentence, do not say or write these expressions.

## Practice

Cross out *like* and *you know* when they are used incorrectly. Write **C** after each correct sentence.

1. Chaco Canyon is not like any other place.     C

2. It is a group of ruins of old dwellings from, like, a thousand years ago.     _____

3. If you like the cliff dwellings at Mesa Verde in Arizona, you know you'll love the ruins in Chaco Canyon.     C

4. Chaco Canyon is in the, you know, northwestern part of New Mexico.     _____

5. Did you know that Chaco Canyon is now a national park?     C

6. Tourists can climb on the, you know, ruins and go into the rooms.     _____

7. You will be surprised at how little you know about the people who once lived there.     C

8. So far, scientists haven't found any, like, burial sites in Chaco.     _____

9. They do know a lot about the people and what they were like.     C

10. The more you know about this mystery, the more you want to know.     C

Decide if each sentence is written correctly or incorrectly. Rewrite each incorrect sentence to make it correct.

**11.** Chaco Canyon is, like, twelve miles long and about one-half mile wide.

Chaco Canyon is twelve miles long and about one-half mile wide.

**12.** Do you know about the other interesting places in Chaco Canyon?

**13.** Another, like, D-shaped village there is Chetro Ketl.

Another D-shaped village there is Chetro Ketl.

**14.** One wall of Chetro Ketl is almost 500 feet long and has been standing for, like, 900 years.

One wall of Chetro Ketl is almost 500 feet long and has been standing for 900 years.

**15.** Archaeologists and astronomers together, you know, studied another famous site, Fajade Butte, at Chaco Canyon.

Archaeologists and astronomers together studied another famous site, Fajade Butte, at Chaco Canyon.

**16.** Inside this huge mesa are carvings that look like spirals.

**17.** At noon on the longest day of the year, the sun makes, like, a dagger through the center of the spiral.

At noon on the longest day of the year, the sun makes a dagger through the center of the spiral.

**18.** At noon on the, you know, shortest day of the year, there are sun daggers on both sides of the spiral.

At noon on the shortest day of the year, there are sun daggers on both sides of the spiral.

# Using *Good* or *Bad* to Compare

## Learn

It is hard to predict the weather. Do you think you could do a (**better**) job than your local weather forecaster does? Some people think the **best** way is just to look out the window. There are (**worse**) ways than that to predict the weather. Most weather forecasters get the **worst** criticism even though they don't control the weather.

Circle the two boldfaced words above that compare two people or things. Underline the two boldfaced words that compare more than two people or things.

> Use **better** and **worse** when you compare two people or things. Use **best** and **worst** when you compare three or more people or things. Avoid *gooder, goodest, bestest, more better, worser, worstest, badder,* and *baddest.* These are all nonstandard forms.

## Practice

Write the form of **good** or **bad** that correctly completes each sentence.

1. Satellites help us do a (better/gooder) job of predicting weather than was possible fifty years ago. _____ better

2. Many think Florida has (better/best) winter weather than Minnesota does. _____ better

3. The hurricane that hit Galveston in 1900 was perhaps the (worser/worst) ever to hit the United States. _____ worst

4. Which city has the (worse/worst) weather: Algiers, Hong Kong, or Lima? _____ worst

5. Of El Paso, Portland, and Phoenix, Portland has the (best/bestest) chance of rain in June. _____ best

6. Some people considered 1998 the (worst/worstest) year for weather because of the climate event called El Niño. _____ worst

7. Where is the (gooder/best) place to take shelter in a tornado? _____ best

8. It is (better/best) to take cover in a basement than in a trailer. _____ better

9. Planes can now fly into the eye of the (worse/worst) hurricanes. _____ worst

Rewrite each sentence. Replace the boldfaced word with the correct word.

**10.** Can you do a **bester** job of predicting the weather than your television weather forecaster can?

Can you do a better job of predicting the weather than your television weather forecaster can?

**11.** What is the **goodest** weather for a successful picnic? _____

What is the best weather for a successful picnic?

**12.** Is it **gooder** to wear lightweight clothes to New Mexico in July? _____

Is it better to wear lightweight clothes to New Mexico in July?

**13.** Do you think the weather is **bester** or **worser** this week than it was last week?

Do you think the weather is better or worse this week than it was last week?

**14.** The survivors of the storm said it was the **worse** one they had ever seen.

The survivors of the storm said it was the worst one they had ever seen.

**15.** Even the **bestest** weather can change in an instant. _____

Even the best weather can change in an instant.

**16.** Last summer we were picnicking when the weather suddenly got **worst**.

Last summer we were picnicking when the weather suddenly got worse.

**17.** We did our **bestest** to get out of the rain. _____

We did our best to get out of the rain.

**18.** We all got wet, but it could have been **worser**. _____

We all got wet, but it could have been worse.

# That, Which, Who

## Learn

Mount Everest is one of the mountains **that** form the Himalaya Mountains. Mount Everest, **which** rises 5.5 miles above sea level, is the highest mountain in the world. It is believed that the first men **who** climbed Mount Everest were Sir Edmund Hillary and Tenzing Norgay.

Which boldfaced word refers to people? _____who_____

> Use **who** to refer to people. Use **which** to refer to things. You may use **that** to refer either to people or to things. Use *that* instead of *which* to begin a clause that is necessary to the meaning of the sentence.

## Practice

Circle the word in parentheses that correctly completes each sentence.

1. Mountains are often the landforms (which/**that**) separate states and countries.

2. The Himalaya Mountains form the boundary (who/**that**) separates India and China.

3. Mount Everest, (**which**/who) is located on the border between Tibet and Nepal, is the highest mountain in the world.

4. Mount Everest is named for Sir George Everest, (which/**who**) was a British surveyor of India in the nineteenth century.

5. The mountain (which/**that**) is called K2 is the second highest mountain in the world.

6. K2, (**which**/that) is located in northern Kashmir, is 28,250 feet above sea level.

7. Both Mount Everest and K2 are part of the same mountain range, the Himalayas, (who/**that**) stretches across southern Asia.

8. The third-highest mountain in the world, (**which**/that) is also in the Himalaya Mountains, is Mount Kanchenjunga (kuhn·chuhn·**jung**·guh).

9. It is believed that the first people to reach the top of Mount Kanchenjunga were part of a British expedition (which/**that**) climbed the mountain in 1955.

10. Many climbers (which/**who**) have attempted to climb these mountains have failed.

Write complete sentences by combining a sentence part from Column 1 with a sentence part from Column 2.

**Column 1**

Kilimanjaro, the highest peak in Africa, inspired Ernest Hemingway,

The highest mountain in Japan is Mount Fuji,

Mount St. Helens is a volcano well known by people

The highest island peak in the world is Mauna Kea,

The second-highest mountain in the world is the one

**Column 2**

which is about 60 miles west of Tokyo.

who wrote the short story "The Snows of Kilimanjaro."

that has the unusual name K2.

who remember that it erupted in 1980.

which is on the island of Hawaii.

11. Kilimanjaro, the highest peak in Africa, inspired Ernest Hemingway, who wrote the short story _____

"The Snows of Kilimanjaro." _____

12. The highest mountain in Japan is Mount Fuji, which is about 60 miles west of Tokyo. _____

_____

13. Mount St. Helens is a volcano well known by people who remember that it erupted in 1980. _____

_____

14. The highest island peak in the world is Mauna Kea, which is on the island of Hawaii. _____

_____

15. The second-highest mountain in the world is the one that has the unusual name K2. _____

_____

# *Real* and *Very*

## Learn

   **a.** The location of rivers is **very** important to transportation.
   **b.** Rivers are **real** valuable to agriculture.      **c.** They are also a **real** source of energy.

In which sentence, **a.**, **b.**, or **c.**, is the boldfaced word used incorrectly? _____**b.**_____

> **Real** is an adjective and must describe a noun or a pronoun. It means "actual." **Very** is an adverb. It means "extremely." Do not use *real* in place of *very*.

## Practice

Draw an **X** through each boldfaced word that is used incorrectly. Write **C** next to each sentence that uses the boldfaced word correctly.

   1.  The Nile River in Africa is a **very** long river, the longest in the world. _____C_____

   2.  The Amazon River in South America is **real** long, too, and it's the next longest. _____

   3.  The plants and animals that can be seen along the riverbanks are **very** interesting. _____C_____

   4.  One **real** benefit of the Nile River is the irrigation it provides Egypt and Sudan. _____C_____

   5.  For many years the source of the Nile River was a **real** mystery to geographers. _____C_____

   6.  Now we know that it flows partly from a **very** large lake named Lake Victoria. _____C_____

   7.  However, the **real** source of the Nile seemed to be the Ruvironza River in Burundi. _____C_____

   8.  The source of the Amazon River lies **real** high in the Andes Mountains of Peru. _____

   9.  The Amazon River carries a **very** large quantity of water through Peru and Brazil. _____C_____

   10. The river basin along the Amazon is **real** important because it has the world's largest tropical rain forest. _____

   11. The loss of the rain forest would be a **real** threat to Earth's environment. _____C_____

   12. The Amazon climate is **very** hot and humid, averaging about 85 degrees. _____C_____

Use facts from the box to write six sentences about the rivers. Use **very** or **real** in each sentence you write. **Answers will vary.**

> The Danube River in Europe inspired Strauss to write the waltz "On the Beautiful Blue Danube."
>
> The Ganges River in India and Bangladesh is considered sacred by many.
>
> The Delaware River became famous when Washington and his troops crossed it in 1776.
>
> The St. Lawrence River in North America is important for transportation.
>
> The Amazon River is an amazing six miles wide at some points.
>
> A well-known sight on the Niagara River in North America is Niagara Falls.

13. _____

_____

14. _____

_____

15. _____

_____

16. _____

_____

17. _____

_____

18. _____

_____

# Set and Sit

## Learn

The teacher **set** her book on the desk. Then she was ready to **sit** down and begin the lesson.

Which boldfaced verb means "placed something somewhere"? _____ set

Which boldfaced verb means "move into a chair"? _____ sit

> **Set** and **sit** are different verbs. *Set* takes a direct object and *sit* does not. If you're about to use *set*, ask yourself, "Set what?" If you can't answer that question, use *sit*. Also, remember that you can't *sit* anything down—you must *set* it down. The past-tense form of *sit* is *sat*. *Set* is spelled the same in the present and past tenses.

## Practice

Circle the word in parentheses that correctly completes each sentence. (**1.–7.**)

Ms. Chavez (**set**/sat) her pointer on the tray of the chalkboard. She explained that she would ask students to answer some questions. They would answer them from where they (set/**sat**) in the classroom. Later they would come to the map and use the pointer.

"Julian," she asked, "what is the long river that divides the United States?"

Julian (set/**sat**) quietly in his seat. He (**set**/sat) his book aside and tried to think of the answer. Then he (set/**sat**) up, leaned forward, and replied loudly, "It's the Mississippi River! It's the longest river in the United States. Its length is over 2,000 miles, and it flows from—"

"Thank you, Julian," Ms. Chavez said with a smile. "Now, Amelia," she continued, "you may come to the map. (**Set**/Sit) the tip of the pointer on the mouth of the Mississippi River."

Amelia rushed to the front of the room and pointed to the northern part of Minnesota. Now Julian couldn't (**sit**/set) still any longer, and he raised his hand. He knew that Amelia was pointing to the source of the river, not the mouth.

Rewrite each sentence. Add a form of **set** or **sit** to complete the sentence correctly. If the word you add begins a sentence, be sure to capitalize it.

**8.** "_____ here, on the west bank of the Mississippi," said the tour director. _____

"Sit here, on the west bank of the Mississippi," said the tour director.

**9.** "As you _____ here, you will be looking at the state of Illinois," she said. _____

As you sit here, you will be looking at the state of Illinois," she said.

**10.** The sound of the old-fashioned calliope _____ the mood for our upcoming trip down the great river.

The sound of the old-fashioned calliope set the mood for our upcoming trip down the great river.

**11.** When we finally boarded the riverboat, I _____ close to the bow. _____

When we finally boarded the riverboat, I sat close to the bow.

**12.** We all _____ quietly on the deck of the riverboat waiting for it to get under way.

We all sat quietly on the deck of the riverboat waiting for it to get under way.

**13.** Mandy _____ her chair beside mine. _____

Mandy set her chair beside mine.

**14.** It was such a beautiful day that I thought, "I could _____ in this place forever."

It was such a beautiful day that I thought, "I could sit in this place forever."

**15.** Two muskrats _____ on the bank and stared at us as we passed by. _____

Two muskrats sat on the bank and stared at us as we passed by.

**16.** At the end of the ride, I _____ my mind on another trip down the Mississippi. _____

At the end of the ride, I set my mind on another trip down the Mississippi.

# Irregular Verbs: *Know* and *Grow*

## Learn

American agriculture has **growed** into an important source of food for the world.
A successful farmer must **know** about soil, seeds, and irrigation.

Which boldfaced verb is correct? _____ know _____

Write the correct form of the incorrect word. _____ grown _____

> **Know** and **grow** are **irregular verbs**. You cannot make the past tense or the past participle of these verbs by adding *-ed*. These verbs have different forms.
>
> | Present Tense | Past Tense | Past Participle (with *have, has,* or *had*) |
> |---|---|---|
> | know(s) | knew | known |
> | grow(s) | grew | grown |

## Practice

Underline the verb in parentheses that correctly completes each sentence.

1. People have (knowed/known) the importance of agriculture to human survival for centuries.

2. Early humans ate whatever (grew/growed) naturally nearby.

3. They (knew/knewed) that when the food ran out, they would have to move to a new area.

4. It took years before people (knowed/knew) how to develop the best plants.

5. Even then, they (knew/knewed) it would take a lot of work and time before food was produced.

6. Some plants (grew/growed) faster and provided more food if water was available.

7. Soon communities had (growed/grown) in places where water was plentiful.

8. The world had never (knowed/known) such a sudden change in the way people lived.

9. The use of modern farm machinery meant farmers now (grew/grown) more food than their own families needed.

10. No one could have (knowed/known) or guessed the changes these machines would make in the life of a family.

Write a sentence to answer each of these questions. Use a form of **know** or **grow** in each answer and do not use *did*. **Answers will vary.**

**11.** Did you know that farmers produce nearly all of the world's food? _____

_____

**12.** How long has corn been growing in American fields? _____

_____

**13.** Did you know how to answer the last question? _____

_____

**14.** Do you know about the hunters and gatherers? _____

_____

**15.** When did you know that agriculture was important for food production? _____

_____

**16.** Did you know anything about farming before you read these sentences? _____

_____

**17.** How long have these flowers been growing in your garden? _____

_____

**18.** Did you know that the United States is a leading grower of soybeans? _____

_____

**19.** Did you grow flowers in your garden before this year? _____

_____

**20.** When did you first know about the importance of farm machinery? _____

_____

# Learn and Teach

## Learn

Today we **learned** about the United States highway system. A state trooper **taught** us that many highways follow old wagon trails.

Which boldfaced word means "gained knowledge"? _____learned_____

Which boldfaced word means "gave knowledge"? _____taught_____

> Both **learn** and **teach** are related to knowledge, so they are often confused. *Learn* means "to get knowledge," and *teach* means "to give knowledge."

## Practice

Circle the word in parentheses that correctly completes each sentence.

1. Our class (**learned**/taught) that the federal interstate highway system covers over 45,000 miles.

2. Studying the highway system can (learn/**teach**) us about how goods move across the nation.

3. One thing it (learned/**taught**) me was that the numbers given to highways are meaningful.

4. Officer Malloy (learned/**taught**) us that most highways with even numbers go east and west, and most highways with odd numbers go north and south.

5. I wondered who (learned/**taught**) Officer Malloy so many things about highways.

6. We also (**learned**/taught) that the U.S. federal highway signs are on black-and-white shields.

7. Maps (learned/**taught**) us that red, white, and blue shields mark the interstate highways.

8. Next, Officer Malloy (learned/**taught**) us about interstate highways with three-digit numbers.

9. I was surprised to (**learn**/teach) that these go around cities instead of through them.

10. One classmate researched famous highways and (learned/**taught**) us what she had learned.

11. From her we (**learned**/taught) about the old federal highway, Route 66.

Rewrite each sentence. Add a form of **learn** or **teach** to complete each sentence correctly.

**12.** One interesting highway we have ____ about is Route 66, which has been renamed or abandoned in many places.

One interesting highway we have learned about is Route 66, which has been renamed or abandoned

in many places.

**13.** Our classmate Jody ____ that Route 66 was planned, by Cyrus Stevens Avery of Tulsa, Oklahoma.

Our classmate Jody learned that Route 66 was planned by Cyrus Stevens Avery of Tulsa, Oklahoma.

**14.** Jody ____ us that Avery was a highway commissioner who developed an interstate highway system.

Jody taught us that Avery was a highway commissioner who developed an interstate

highway system.

**15.** She had also ____ that Route 66 was completed in 1926. _____

She had also learned that Route 66 was completed in 1926.

**16.** Another fact Jody ____ me is that Route 66 linked Chicago with Los Angeles through the Great Plains.

Another fact Jody taught me is that Route 66 linked Chicago with Los Angeles through

the Great Plains.

**17.** If you study a map of old Route 66, you will ____ that it went through eight states.

If you study a map of old Route 66, you will learn that it went through eight states.

**18.** The role Route 66 played in our history ____ us much about the importance of transportation.

The role Route 66 played in our history teaches us much about the importance of transportation.

# Subject and Object Pronouns

## Learn

Our class has reading teams. (We) join teams to read different kinds of books. Charles has joined all of the teams. I joined two of **them**.

Circle the boldfaced word that replaces the phrase *Our class*.

Underline the boldfaced word that replaces the phrase *the teams*.

Which boldfaced word is the subject of a sentence? _____We_____

> A pronoun can be the subject or the object in a sentence. **Subject pronouns** include *I, he, she, we,* and *they*. **Object pronouns** can be used after an action verb or a preposition. Object pronouns include *me, him, her, us,* and *them*. The pronouns *it* and *you* can be either subjects or objects.

## Practice

Circle each boldfaced word that is a subject pronoun. Underline each boldfaced word that is an object pronoun.

1. Our library has many great books. (I) have read many of **them**.

2. The reading teams help **us** learn to appreciate all kinds of literature.

3. Charles reads all the time. (He) likes many different types of books.

4. Melinda also reads a lot of books. (She) likes fiction best.

5. Charles told **her** to try science fiction next time.

6. Charles asked Melinda and **me** to join the science fiction reading team.

7. Melinda is good at science, and (she) enjoys reading about **it**.

8. Charles picked the books for **us** to read. (We) took them home.

9. Now Charles wants Melinda and **me** to read about science.

10. (You) might like both science and science fiction.

Rewrite each sentence. Replace each boldfaced word or phrase with a pronoun.

11. **Melinda** read five books with the science fiction reading team. _____

    She read five books with the science fiction reading team.

12. **Melinda and I** read **the five books** together. _____

    We read them together.

13. A favorite book for **Melinda and me** was Madeleine L'Engle's <u>A Wrinkle in Time</u>.

    A favorite book for us was Madeleine L'Engle's <u>A Wrinkle in Time.</u>

14. Charles and Melinda read <u>**A Wrinkle in Time**</u> twice. _____

    Charles and Melinda read it twice.

15. **Charles and Melinda** liked the characters of Mrs. Whatsit and Mrs. Who.

    They liked the characters of Mrs. Whatsit and Mrs. Who.

16. **Charles and Melinda** wanted to read more about **Mrs. Whatsit and Mrs. Who.**

    They wanted to read more about them.

17. I agreed with **Melinda** that we should join the fiction team next. _____

    I agreed with her that we should join the fiction team next.

18. **The fiction team members** might include science fiction in their choices, too.

    They might include science fiction in their choices, too.

19. I think I have read enough of **science fiction** for a while, though. _____

    I think I have read enough of it for a while, though.

20. I might ask **the members of the fiction team** to also choose historical fiction.

    I might ask them to also choose historical fiction.

# Pronouns in Pairs

## Learn

   **a.** Josh and me decided to read books to the third graders.

   **b.** Then Josh and I chose some books by Patricia C. McKissack.

If you take out "Josh and" from each sentence, which sentence, **a.** or **b.,** sounds correct? __**b.**__

> Use the pronouns *I, we, he, she,* and *they* as **subjects** in sentences. Use
> the pronouns *me, us, him, her,* and *them* as **objects** in sentences.

## Practice

Circle the correct pronoun in each sentence. Write **S** after the sentence if you chose a subject pronoun. Write **O** if you chose an object pronoun.

1.  The second graders asked Josh and (I/**me**) to read *Flossie and the Fox.*     O

2.  (**He**/Him) and I got the book from the library.     S

3.  Josh and (**I**/me) had read the book many times before.     S

4.  Fifth graders read books to our teacher and (we/**us**) when we were in second grade.     O

5.  My twin sister and (**I**/me) got several good books for our birthday.     S

6.  One thing the second graders liked about Flossie was the picture of the fox and (she/**her**) on the cover.     O

7.  The way (**she**/her) and the fox are grinning gives the readers a clue to the story.     S

8.  The students listened to Josh and (I/**me**) read every word.     O

9.  (**He**/Him) and I read as if we were the characters of Flossie and the fox.     S

10. The students enjoyed the conversation between Flossie and (he/**him**).     O

11. (**She**/Her) and the fox have very different ways of speaking.     S

12. The class clapped their hands for Josh and (I/**me**) when we finished.     O

## Apply

Rewrite each sentence. Substitute a pronoun for each boldfaced noun or noun phrase.

13. Sandra and **Kevin** read other books by Patricia C. McKissack. _____

    Sandra and he read other books by Patricia C. McKissack.

14. The librarian found the books for **Sandra and Kevin**. _____

    The librarian found the books for them.

15. **Ms. Knowles** and **Kevin** selected <u>Mirandy and Brother Wind</u> to read to the second graders.

    She and he selected <u>Mirandy and Brother Wind</u> to read to the second graders.

16. Ms. Knowles asked **Kevin** and **Sandra** to take turns reading the book aloud first. _____

    Ms. Knowles asked him and her to take turns reading the book aloud first.

17. **Sandra** and Kevin like other books by Patricia McKissack and Fredrick McKissack.

    She and Kevin like other books by Patricia McKissack and Fredrick McKissack.

18. **Patricia McKissack** and **Fredrick McKissack** have written books on many subjects.

    She and he have written books on many subjects.

19. My class likes the biographies by **Patricia and Fredrick McKissack**. _____

    My class likes the biographies by them.

20. **Patricia McKissack and Fredrick McKissack** did extensive research about Wilma Rudolph and W.E.B. Du Bois.

    They did extensive research about Wilma Rudolph and W.E.B. Du Bois.

21. **Kevin** and **Sandra** liked the biographies about them. _____

    He and she liked the biographies about them.

22. They wrote reports on **Wilma Rudolph** and **W.E.B. Du Bois**. _____

    They wrote reports on her and him.

# Using *I* or *Me*

## Learn

**a.** Me and Briana like to read biographies.
**b.** The librarian gave her and me some books to read.

In which sentence, **a.** or **b.**, are pronouns used correctly? ___b.___

> **I** is a subject pronoun. It can be used as the subject of a sentence. **Me** is an object pronoun. It is used after an action verb or a preposition. When you talk or write about yourself and another person, always name the other person first.

## Practice

Underline the group of words in parentheses that will complete each sentence correctly.

1. (Briana and I/Me and Briana) decided to read *Profiles in Courage* by John F. Kennedy.

2. It had biographies of people that interested (she and I/her and me).

3. Briana thought the biographies were of people like (she and I/her and me).

4. (I and she/She and I) have a lot of courage, but we're not like the people in the book.

5. (Her and I/She and I) read about Daniel Webster and Thomas Hart Benton.

6. Then (me and the librarian/the librarian and I) looked for another book.

7. (He and I/I and him) walked between the stacks of books.

8. Briana followed (me and him/him and me) when she had finished reading.

9. Mr. Jamieson asked (Briana and me/Briana and I) if we still wanted a biography.

10. (She and me/She and I) said we would like biographies about women this time.

11. Finally, (Briana and me/Briana and I) found a book we wanted to read.

12. Now (me and her/she and I) are reading *Babe Didrikson: Athlete of the Century* by Rozanne Knudson.

*Strategies for Writers—Conventions & Skills Practice*  **Unit 4**

# Apply

Imagine that you are visiting the library with a friend. Rewrite each sentence so it refers to you and your friend. Use your friend's name in some sentences and replace your friend's name with a pronoun in other sentences. Remember to use a capital letter to begin a sentence.

13. _____ and _____ looked for biographies. _____

    **Tina and I looked for biographies.**

14. The librarian suggested that _____ and _____ also look for autobiographies. _____

    **The librarian suggested that she and I also look for autobiographies.**

15. _____ and _____ asked what the difference is between biographies and autobiographies.

    **Jonah and I asked what the difference is between biographies and autobiographies.**

16. Ms. Han told _____ and _____ that autobiographies are stories of a person's life written by that person.

    **Ms. Han told him and me that autobiographies are stories of a person's life written by that person.**

17. _____ and _____ decided to try an autobiography. _____

    **Tina and I decided to try an autobiography.**

18. Ms. Han had a suggestion for _____ and _____. _____

    **Ms. Han had a suggestion for her and me.**

19. Now _____ and _____ are reading <u>The Moon and I</u> by Betsy Byars. _____

    **Now she and I are reading <u>The Moon and I</u> by Betsy Byars.**

20. Our friend Jamal told _____ and _____ that it was a book about the moon. _____

    **Our friend Jamal told her and me that it was a book about the moon.**

21. "You should never judge a book by its title," _____ and _____ told him. _____

    **"You should never judge a book by its title," she and I told him.**

22. Later _____ and _____ will tell Jamal that Moon is a snake. _____

    **Later she and I will tell Jamal that Moon is a snake.**

# Pronoun Antecedents

## Learn

My favorite poem is by Robert Frost. **It** has the line "And that has made all the difference."

Underline the phrase that the boldfaced pronoun replaces.

> An **antecedent** is the word or phrase a pronoun replaces. The antecedent always includes a noun. When you write a pronoun, be sure its antecedent is clear. Pronouns must also **agree** with their antecedents. An antecedent and a pronoun agree when they have the same number (singular or plural) and gender (masculine, feminine, or neuter).

## Practice

Underline the **antecedent** for each boldfaced **pronoun**. The antecedent may be one word or more than one word.

1. When I read a good poem, I think about **it** all day long.

2. Our class reads poetry on Mondays. **We** read by ourselves or as a group.

3. When we get to choose a poet, I choose Robert Frost. **He** wrote many poems about nature.

4. Frost was awarded the Pulitzer Prize for his poetry four times. **It** is one of the most important awards for writers.

5. When John F. Kennedy was inaugurated as President in 1961, **he** asked Robert Frost to read one of his poems.

6. In "The Road Not Taken," Frost tells of two roads in the woods. He writes that he was sorry he could not travel on both of **them**.

7. At the end of the poem, Frost says **he** took the road "less traveled by."

8. Poetry really makes me think. **It** uses only a few words to express big ideas.

Read the first sentence. Then rewrite the second sentence adding a pronoun for the boldfaced word or words in the first sentence.

9. I read a **book of poetry** yesterday. _____ was about dogs. _____

   It was about dogs.
   _____

10. All the **poems** in Good Dog Poems are about dogs. _____ were written by many writers.

    They were written by many writers.
    _____

    _____

11. **Ogden Nash** wrote about how lovable dogs are. _____ wrote, "A wet dog is the lovingest."

    He wrote, "A wet dog is the lovingest."
    _____

    _____

12. Myra Livingston wrote about **dogs,** too. She says _____ love to go out in the rain.

    She says they love to go out in the rain.
    _____

    _____

13. Another poet I like is **Eve Merriam**. _____ uses the sounds of words in interesting ways.

    She uses the sounds of words in interesting ways.
    _____

    _____

14. In "How to Eat a Poem," she says not to be polite with **a poem**. We should bite into _____.

    We should bite into it.
    _____

    _____

15. Both **David McCord and Robert Frost** have written poems about climbing trees.
    _____ must have loved to climb trees themselves.

    They must have loved to climb trees themselves.
    _____

    _____

16. **Poems** are fun to read. I read _____ every chance I get. _____

    I read them every chance I get.
    _____

# Making the Subject and Verb Agree

## Learn

(One) of our book **clubs** reads only plays.

Circle the boldfaced noun that is the simple subject.
Underline the boldfaced noun that is the object of the preposition *of*.

Is the subject singular or plural? ____singular____

Write the verb. ____reads____

> The **subject** and its **verb must agree**. Add -*s* or -*es* to a regular verb in the
> present tense when the subject is a singular noun or *he, she,* or *it*. Do not
> add -*s* or -*es* to a regular verb in the present tense when the subject is a
> plural noun or *I, you, we,* or *they*. Be sure that the verb agrees with its
> subject and not with the object of a preposition that comes before the verb.

## Practice

Underline the simple subject in each sentence. Circle the correct verb in parentheses.

1. Six members on Julie's team ((want)/wants) to read four plays.

2. They ((agree)/agrees) to perform one of the plays for the class.

3. This book about plays (tell/(tells)) how to put on a class play.

4. The plays in this book ((include)/includes) one called *Who Goes There?*

5. This play, like most plays, (divide/(divides)) events into acts and scenes.

6. The seven characters in the play ((appear)/appears) at different times.

7. A list of props (provide/(provides)) information about the things needed on stage.

8. Drawings of the settings (follows/(follow)) the list of props.

9. They ((show)/shows) the placement of furniture, doors, and tables.

10. Our group of players ((plans)/plan) to have a narrator explain the settings.

# Apply

Write a verb to complete each sentence correctly. You may use a verb from the pairs in the Word Bank. You may use a verb more than once.

## Word Bank

| | | | |
|---|---|---|---|
| gives/give | suggests/suggest | likes/like | knows/know |
| stands/stand | shows/show | needs/need | says/say |
| takes/take | agrees/agree | draws/draw | makes/make |

11. Jeremy's book _____ gives _____ instructions for making stage sets.

12. The instructions _____ show _____ wooden platforms for the stage.

13. Jeremy's mother _____ likes _____ to do carpentry, so we _____ agree _____ to ask her to help with the platforms.

14. The platforms _____ stand _____ at different heights.

15. Each one _____ shows _____ where a different scene takes place.

16. We also _____ need _____ scenery because one scene of our play is in a forest.

17. Serina said she will help because she _____ takes _____ an art class.

18. All the students in the art class _____ say _____ they will help.

19. While one student _____ makes _____ pencil sketches of the forest, other students will get out the paints.

20. The art students _____ suggest _____ adding more color to the set.

21. Serina's father _____ likes _____ to help make lighting boxes.

22. The students in my class _____ know _____ how to read their lines.

23. We _____ like _____ learning our lines and making stage sets.

24. All the teachers in the school _____ say _____ that the play will be a success.

25. All the students _____ agree _____ that the hard work will really pay off.

# Forms of *Be*

## Learn

  **a.** Some plays **are** full of make-believe characters.

  **b.** My favorite play **is** *Jack and the Beanstalk.*

Which sentence, **a.** or **b.**, has a singular subject? ___b.___

What is the boldfaced verb in that sentence? ___is___

Which sentence, **a.** or **b.**, has a plural subject? ___a.___

What is the boldfaced verb in that sentence? ___are___

> *Am, is, was, are,* and *were* are forms of the verb **be**. Use *am* after the pronoun *I*. Use *is* or *was* after a **singular subject** or after the pronouns *he, she,* or *it*. Use *are* or *were* after a **plural subject** or after the pronouns *we, you,* or *they.*

## Practice

Circle the form of **be** that completes each sentence correctly.

1. Plays (is/**are**) often about familiar topics.

2. One popular kind of play (**is**/are) fantasy, a story that couldn't really happen.

3. Cass (**is**/are) a member of the drama club.

4. She (**was**/were) the club member who got the idea of writing a play.

5. The members of her club (is/**are**) writing a play and planning to perform it for us.

6. *Ring the Bells!* (**is**/are) the name of the play.

7. The setting of the play (**is**/are) mainly inside a house in a village.

8. Some scenes in the play (is/**are**) in a forest nearby.

9. Years ago, bells (was/**were**) useful for sending messages.

10. The bells (is/**are**) in the forest, but no one has ever seen them.

# Apply

Write a form of the verb *be* from the Word Bank to complete each sentence in the play correctly. Remember to capitalize the first word in a sentence.

## Word Bank

am     is     was     were     are

### Ring the Bells!

11. **Harry:**    When _____was_____ the last time the bells rang?

12. **Hester:**    _____Was_____ it in December a long time ago?

13. **Harry:**    Yes, it _____was_____ more than ten years ago.

14. **Hester:**    How do you know? You _____were_____ only ten years old!

15. **Harry:**    I _____am_____ very smart, and I read a lot.

16. **Hortense:** Where _____were_____ you, Hester, when the bells rang last?

17. **Hester:**    That _____is_____ none of your business, but I _____was_____ playing with my apple doll in the forest.

18. **Horace:**    _____Are_____ you sure? We _____were_____ looking all over

 for you. You _____were_____ only three years old then.

19. **Hester:**    (*Looking at Harry*) I _____was_____ very smart when I _____was_____ three years old.

20. **Hortense:** Don't argue, children. There _____is_____ a saying that the bells will not ring when children are arguing.

21. **Horace:**    (*To himself*) Then how _____is_____ it possible that they ever rang?

22. **Horace:**    What _____is_____ that I hear? I think the bells _____are_____ ringing!

(*Everyone stares toward the forest. Hortense walks to the telephone on the desk and picks it up.*)

**Hortense:** Hello! Hello! We have been waiting for you to call.

(*Curtain*)

# Verb Tense

## Learn

I **am reading** a book about Native American art. I **will learn** a lot about pottery and blankets. My teacher **suggests** the book to me last week.

Which boldfaced verb does not give a correct sense of time? _____ *suggests* _____

> All the words in a sentence must work together to give an accurate sense of time. Make sure each **verb** is in the **proper tense** for the time period being discussed.

## Practice

Circle the verb or verb phrase that gives the correct sense of time.

1. A week ago, our class (finish/finished) reading *The Pueblo* by Charlotte and David Yue.

2. By reading this book, we (find/found) out about the pueblo villages of the Southwest.

3. *The Pueblo* (has/will have) beautiful illustrations of the people and their pueblos.

4. Some chapters (included/include) descriptions of life in the pueblo communities.

5. According to this book, many of the pueblos (are abandoned/were abandoned) hundreds of years ago.

6. The word *pueblo* (refers/had referred) to the type of houses as well as to the villages.

7. Tomorrow, each member of our class (wrote/will write) a report about something learned from the book.

8. I quickly (decided/have decided) to write about the style of the pueblo home.

9. The first-floor rooms of these homes (build/were built) below ground.

10. In the abandoned pueblos, it is these lower levels that still (exist/will exist) today.

11. The authors (have written/had written) an interesting chapter about pueblo life today.

12. This informational book (tells/will tell) about the past but also about the present.

Rewrite each sentence. Use the verb and verb tense in parentheses.

**13.** David Macaulay (write, past) a book called <u>Castle</u> about the building of a castle.

David Macaulay wrote a book called <u>Castle</u> about the building of a castle.

**14.** This make-believe castle (to be, past) in Wales in the thirteenth century. _____

This make-believe castle was in Wales in the thirteenth century.

**15.** Macaulay (make, present) this castle seem real. _____

Macaulay makes this castle seem real.

**16.** According to the book, a king, a lord, and a master engineer (decide, past) to build a castle.

According to the book, a king, a lord, and a master engineer decided to build a castle.

**17.** The master engineer and his staff (plan, past) all of the castle grounds. _____

The master engineer and his staff planned all of the castle grounds.

**18.** The grounds (include, past) the moat, gatehouses, apartments, great hall, shops, and inner yard.

The grounds included the moat, gatehouses, apartments, great hall, shops, and inner yard.

**19.** On one page, Macaulay (show, present) the master engineer's diagram of the castle grounds.

On one page, Macaulay shows the master engineer's diagram of the castle grounds.

**20.** The book (provide, present) a diagram of the town as well. _____

The book provides a diagram of the town as well.

**21.** By studying this book, I (find, past) out just how castles are built. _____

By studying this book, I found out just how castles are built.

**22.** This book (entertain, present) as well as informs this reader. _____

This book entertains as well as informs this reader.

# Negatives

## Learn

**a.** Sheryl said she hadn't never read anything as funny as that book.

**b.** It wasn't meant to be a funny book, though.

Which sentence, **a.** or **b.**, has two negative words? _____a._____

> A **negative** is a word that means "no" or "not." The words *no, not, nothing, none, never, nowhere,* and *nobody* are negatives. The negative word *not* is often found in contractions like *don't* or *wasn't*. Use only one negative word in a sentence to express a negative idea.

## Practice

Circle the negative words in these sentences. Write **X** after each sentence that has two negative expressions.

1. Ari said he (wasn't) going to read (no) more serious books for a while. ___X___

2. "You (don't) (never) read anything serious, anyway," said his friend Stephan. ___X___

3. Ari said he (hadn't) had (no) fun reading lately. ___X___

4. Stephan said, "I'll bet you (can't) resist this book." _____

5. The book *How to Talk to Your Cat* (wasn't) (no) big book. ___X___

6. "You (can't) (never) talk to a cat," Ari protested. ___X___

7. "You (won't) (never) know until you read this book," Stephan responded. ___X___

8. Ari thought the square book (didn't) look (nothing) like a regular book. ___X___

9. He (hadn't) ever heard of the author, Patricia Moyes. _____

10. Stephan said his mother told him Patricia Moyes (didn't) usually write cat books. _____

11. Ari picked up the book, and then he (couldn't) put it down. _____

12. He (hadn't) (never) realized that cats could be so interesting. ___X___

Rewrite the **Practice** sentences that have two negatives correctly. There is more than one way to correct each sentence. **Answers will vary. Possible responses appear below.**

13. Ari said he wasn't going to read any more serious books for a while.

14. "You never read anything serious, anyway," said his friend Stephan.

15. Ari said he'd had no fun reading lately.

16. The book How to Talk to Your Cat wasn't a big book.

17. "You can't talk to a cat," Ari protested.

18. "You'll never know until you read this book," Stephan responded.

19. Ari thought the square book looked nothing like a regular book.

20. He had never realized that cats could be so interesting.

Copyright © Zaner-Bloser, Inc.

# Comparative and Superlative Adjectives

## Learn

My reading team is **larger** than your team. We are reading one of the **most famous** tales of all time, "Sleeping Beauty."

Which boldfaced adjective compares two things? _____larger_____

Which boldfaced adjective compares more than two things? _____most famous_____

> The **comparative form** of an **adjective** compares two people, places, or things. It is often followed by the word *than*. Add *-er* to short adjectives to create the comparative form. Use the word *more* before long adjectives. The **superlative form** of an adjective compares three or more people, places, or things. The superlative form usually follows the article *the*. Add *-est* to short adjectives to create the superlative. Use the word *most* before long adjectives.

## Practice

Decide how many things are being compared in each sentence. Then circle the correct form of the adjective in parentheses.

1. The events in folktales are often the (stranger/**strangest**) things anyone can imagine.

2. Each new event seems (**stranger**/strangest) than the one before.

3. The Russian tale *I-Know-Not-What, I-Know-Not-Where*, adapted by Eric A. Kimmel in a picture book, is told by the (smarter/**smartest**) dove one could ever meet.

4. A simple archer becomes (**more powerful**/most powerful) than the rich czar.

5. During the adventures, the archer has to solve the (harder/**hardest**) riddles a frog can invent.

6. The frog tells the archer that the (importantest/**most important**) thing to remember is to be afraid of nothing.

7. Only the dove is (**wiser**/wisest) than the strange character named Nobody.

8. Eventually, the dove turns into the (more beautiful/**most beautiful**) woman in the world.

9. At the end, the archer says that he is the (happier/**happiest**) person that ever lived.

10. Some of the (famousest/**most famous**) stories are based on folktales.

Write the correct form of the adjective in parentheses. Add **more, most, -er,** or **-est** where needed.

11. Myths, legends, and tales about the objects in the sky and events on Earth are among

the _____ most interesting _____ stories ever told. (interesting)

12. The book *Sun, Moon, and Stars* by Mary Hoffman and Jane Ray has some of the

_____ most famous _____ stories about objects in the sky. (famous)

13. The authors explain that for years the sky was the _____ most reliable _____ map
people had. (reliable)

14. The book retells a myth from Latvia that explains why the moon is _____ fuller _____
at some times than at other times. (full)

15. A myth from the Mayan culture tells that the sun is actually a god. This god was

_____ braver _____ than another god who wanted to be the sun. (brave)

16. The same myth says that the other god finally became the moon. The sun, however, is

always _____ brighter _____ than the moon. (bright)

17. A Hindu legend explains how elephants were made to respect hares, who were much

_____ smaller _____ creatures than elephants. (small)

18. One of the _____ most beautiful _____ goddesses in Greek mythology was Aphrodite.
(beautiful)

19. In Irish mythology, fish are among the _____ most knowledgeable _____ creatures.
(knowledgeable)

20. A tale from Japan tells how the _____ richest _____ man in the land learns
that true wealth is found in family and in nature. (rich)

21. One of the _____ best known _____ legends is that of Johnny Appleseed, a
real person who planted apple trees across the United States and befriended every
person and animal he met along the way. (well known)

22. Myths and legends and tales often explain the _____ most mysterious _____ things
on Earth and in the sky. (mysterious)

# Comparative and Superlative Adverbs

## Learn

a. In science class, we handled the vinegar **more carefully** than the water.

b. We handled the ammonia **most carefully** of all the materials.

Which sentence, **a.** or **b.**, has a boldfaced adverb that compares two actions? **a.**

Which sentence, **a.** or **b.**, has a boldfaced adverb that compares three or more actions? **b.**

> **Adverbs** that end in *-ly* are preceded by *more* for the **comparative** form (*more carefully*) and are often followed by the word *than*. Adverbs that end in *-ly* are preceded by *most* for the **superlative** form (*most carefully*). Some adverbs add *-er* for the comparative form (*faster*) and *-est* for the superlative form (*fastest*).

## Practice

Circle the correct form of the adverb in each of these sentences.

1. Adrienne said she could (**more easily**/most easily) read books about science experiments than books about myths and legends.

2. The librarian showed Adrienne how to find the books she wanted (**more rapidly**/most rapidly) with the computer catalog than with the card catalog.

3. Renee used the computer (**faster**/fastest) than Adrienne, but she wasn't finding what she wanted.

4. They had been working in the library the (longer/**longest**) of any students in their class.

5. The librarian pointed out how to use the computer (more efficiently/**most efficiently**).

6. Now Adrienne found the book (**more quickly**/most quickly) than before.

7. Adrienne thinks she will visit the library (oftener/**more often**) than she does now.

8. Adrienne admitted that she should have learned about the library computer (**sooner**/more soon).

9. She will use the computer catalog (happier/**more happily**) now.

Complete each sentence by writing the correct form of the adverb in parentheses.
You will need to add **more, most, -er,** or **-est** to each adverb.

10. Of all the books on the subject, *Science Teasers* by Rose Wyler and Eva-Lee Baird

explains things _____**most clearly**_____. (clearly)

11. There are puzzles that you can solve _____**more easily**_____ than a friend
can if you know the science behind the questions. (easily)

12. One puzzle might ask how someone can go around the earth _____**faster**_____
than an astronaut. (fast)

13. Adrienne answered that problem _____**more quickly**_____ than any of her
classmates. (quickly)

14. Someone close to the North or South Pole could get around the world

_____**more swiftly**_____ than an astronaut in space. (swiftly)

15. If two people decided to race around the world, the one standing _____**nearer**_____
the North or South Pole would go the shorter distance. (near)

16. The book presented the puzzles the _____**most cleverly**_____ of any Adrienne had
ever seen. (cleverly)

17. Renee and Adrienne think this book will help them do their science work

_____**more intelligently**_____. (intelligently)

18. Both girls can now search for library books _____**more effectively**_____ than they could
before. (effectively)

19. They will probably arrive at the library _____**earlier**_____ than most of their
friends. (early)

20. Of all the students, you will find them in the library _____**most often**_____. (often)

21. Renee lives _____**farther**_____ from the library than Adrienne. (far)

22. They laughed about which of them dressed the _____**more warmly**_____ for the walk
to the library. (warm)

23. Will they continue going to the library the _____**most frequently**_____ of anyone in their
class? (frequently)

# Writing Sentences Correctly

## Learn

a. Some paintings are created to represent nature and people just as we see them.

b. Have you seen paintings by Rousseau?

c. Look carefully at the people and the details.

d. Imagine the public's surprise at the Cubist movement!

Which sentence makes a statement? ___a.___ Circle its end mark.

Which sentence gives a command? ___c.___ Circle its end mark.

Which sentence asks a question? ___b.___ Circle its end mark.

Which sentence shows excitement? ___d.___ Circle its end mark.

Begin every sentence with a capital letter. A **declarative** sentence makes a statement and ends with a **period**. An **interrogative** sentence asks a question and ends with a **question mark**. An **imperative** sentence gives a command and ends with a **period** or an **exclamation point**. An **exclamatory** sentence shows excitement and ends with an **exclamation point**.

## Practice

Correct any capitalization or punctuation errors in these sentences. Label each sentence **dec** (declarative), **int** (interrogative), **imp** (imperative), or **exc** (exclamatory).

1. Cubism is a style of painting that began in the early twentieth century. ___dec___

2. Why do you think it is called *cubism*? ___int___

3. Cubist paintings made the art critic Louis Vauxcelles think of cubes. ___dec___

4. look closely at a cubist painting and try to see familiar objects. ___imp___

5. Wow, the objects might appear to be scattered all about! ___exc___

6. Some cubist paintings make you think the painter cut up pieces of a painting and then pasted them together in a jumble. ___dec___

7. think about this new idea for a minute. ___imp___

8. why would an artist want it to look that way? ___int___

**Apply**

Rewrite each sentence to make it the kind of sentence named in parentheses. Underline the names of the paintings. **Answers will vary. Possible responses appear below.**

9. Can you find the woman's fingers in Pablo Picasso's Woman Weeping? (imperative)

   Find the woman's fingers in Pablo Picasso's <u>Woman Weeping</u>.

10. Find the tears in the painting. (interrogative)

    Can you find the tears in the painting?

11. Let's look closely at her sad face. (exclamatory)

    What a sad face she has!

12. How long did it take you to find the musical instruments in Picasso's Mandolin and Guitar? (declarative)

    There are musical instruments in Picasso's <u>Mandolin and Guitar</u>.

13. In that painting there are curves, straight lines, and diamond shapes. (interrogative)

    Are there curves, straight lines, and diamond shapes in that painting?

14. How can you tell that the musical instruments are in a house? (declarative)

    You can see that the musical instruments are in a house.

15. Is it difficult to find the man and the guitar in Georges Braque's Man with a Guitar? (declarative)

    It is difficult to find a man and a guitar in Georges Braque's <u>Man with a Guitar</u>.

16. Was the guitar run over by a truck? (exclamatory)

    Wow, the guitar looks run over by a truck!

# Proper Nouns and Proper Adjectives

## Learn

Many artists have been fascinated by the character of <u>Don Quixote</u>, created by <u>Miguel de Cervantes</u> of <u>Spain</u>. Among these artists are <u>Gustave Doré</u>, <u>Richard Strauss</u>, and <u>Graham Greene</u>.

Underline words that name specific people or places.

> A common noun names a person, place, or thing. A **proper noun** names a specific person, place, or thing. All the important words in proper nouns are capitalized. The names of months and days of the week are proper nouns. **Proper adjectives** are descriptive words formed from proper nouns. They must be capitalized. A **title of respect** is used before a person's name. Titles of respect are also capitalized.

## Practice

Underline lowercase letters that should be capital letters. Draw a line through capital letters that should be lowercase letters.

1. Cervantes wrote the first part of his novel about Don Quixote in 1605 and the second Part in 1615.

2. In the novel, Don quixote and his friend Sancho Panza travel about the area of La Mancha in spain performing heroic deeds.

3. In most cases, don quixote and sancho Panza are mistaken about how to help people in la mancha, but they remain Heroes for their good intentions.

4. In 1965, a musical play by Dale wasserman opened in new york City.

5. For this Play, *Man of La mancha*, the music was composed by Mitch Leigh and the lyrics were written by joe Darion.

6. The most popular song from the Production was "The impossible Dream."

7. One of the other musical versions of the story was the work by the german composer richard strauss.

8. Strauss's Classical Work was written in 1897, but a popular recording was made much more recently by the new york Philharmonic Orchestra.

Rewrite these sentences. Correct any errors.

9. The Illustrator Gustave Doré created elaborate illustrations that show the gentle nature of don quixote.

The illustrator Gustave Doré created elaborate illustrations that show the gentle nature of

Don Quixote.

10. Graham greene wrote <u>Monsignor Quixote</u>, a Novel based on the important ideas he found in Cervantes' masterpiece.

Graham Greene wrote <u>Monsignor Quixote</u>, a novel based on the important ideas he found in

Cervantes' masterpiece.

11. woodcarvers, especially those in spain and mexico, have portrayed don quixote.

Woodcarvers, especially those in Spain and Mexico, have portrayed Don Quixote.

12. Several of the heroes of plays by william shakespeare have been the subject of musical compositions.

Several of the heroes of plays by William Shakespeare have been the subject of musical

compositions.

13. The nineteenth-century composers Berlioz, Gounod, and tchaikovsky have all written musical compositions based on <u>Romeo and juliet</u>.

The nineteenth-century composers Berlioz, Gounod, and Tchaikovsky have all written musical

compositions based on <u>Romeo and Juliet</u>.

14. Music for a ballet about romeo and Juliet was created in 1936 by the composer from moscow, Sergei Prokofiev.

Music for a ballet about Romeo and Juliet was created in 1936 by the composer from Moscow,

Sergei Prokofiev.

15. films based on shakespeare's young lovers were made in 1908, 1936, 1954, and 1968.

Films based on Shakespeare's young lovers were made in 1908, 1936, 1954, and 1968.

# Initials and Abbreviations

## Learn

Mr. Brian Lanker photographed many African American women for a special exhibition. On Mon., Feb. 5, Dr. J. Morrell arranged for our class to see the exhibition.

Circle a short way to write *Mister*. Underline a short way to write *Doctor*. Draw a box around short ways to write *Monday* and *February*. Circle a single letter that stands for a name.

> An **abbreviation** is a shortened form of a word. **Titles of respect** are usually abbreviated. So are words in **addresses** such as *Street* (*St.*) and *Avenue* (*Ave.*). **Days,** some **months**, and **kinds of businesses** are often abbreviated in informal notes. Abbreviations usually begin with a capital letter and end with a period. An **initial** takes the place of a name. It is written as a capital letter followed by a period.

## Practice

Circle each lowercase letter that should be a capital letter. Draw a line through each capital letter that should be a lowercase letter. Add periods where they are needed.

1. Mr. Lanker's exhibition and the book of photographs and essays were called *I Dream a World;* the title is taken from a poem by mr. langston hughes.

2. The first photograph is of Ms. Rosa parks, the activist who was born in Alabama.

3. Ms. Eva Jessye, a choral director, tells of meeting Booker t.Washington while in College.

4. Ms Jessye was born on jan 20, 1895, and she tells a moving story about her life.

5. The photograph of Coretta Scott King, the widow of dr. Martin Luther King, Jr., shows her in a thoughtful mood.

6. Mr. Lanker photographed Rep.Shirley Chisholm, the first African American woman to be elected to the u.s. Congress.

7. The photograph of dr.Alexa Canady, a Surgeon, captures her in operating room clothing.

8. A beautiful photograph of a teacher, Ms.Ruby m. forsythe, shows her with two children.

9. Jean b. Hutson worked at the N.Y. Public Library and City College of n.y.

10. Dr. Morrell is taking our Class to the Library on Grant ave. to see the exhibition.

# Apply

Write sentences that include the words in each item below. Use abbreviations and initials.

11. Mister Brian Lanker _____ Mr. B. Lanker
_____

12. New York Public Library _____ N.Y. Public Library
_____

13. Monday through Thursday _____ Mon. through Thurs.
_____

14. Doctor Martin Luther King, Junior _____ Dr. M. L. King, Jr.
_____

15. Representative Kathleen Wilson _____ Rep. K. Wilson
_____

16. Senator Lacey Keene _____ Sen. L. Keene
_____

17. United States Senate _____ U.S. Senate
_____

18. 1600 Pennsylvania Avenue _____ 1600 Pennsylvania Ave.
_____

19. World Photography, Incorporated _____ World Photography, Inc.
_____

20. January 1, 2003 _____ Jan. 1, 2003
_____

21. Professor Jane Schnabel Bakerman _____ Prof. J. S. Bakerman
_____

# Titles

## Learn

Mom and Dad rented the movie <u>The Sound of Music</u>. Saira and I complained because Mom and Dad sang "Do-Re-Mi" for a week! We're going to read <u>Videos for Today and Tomorrow</u> before they rent our next movie.

Write the name of the movie exactly as it is shown. _____ <u>The Sound of Music</u> _____

Write the name of the song. Include the punctuation marks. _____ "Do-Re-Mi" _____

Write the name of the book exactly as it is shown. _____ <u>Videos for Today and Tomorrow</u> _____

> Underline **book titles** and **movie titles**. Use quotation marks around the titles of **songs, stories,** and **poems**. Capitalize the first word and last word in every title you write. Capitalize all other words except articles, prepositions, and conjunctions. Remember to capitalize forms of the verb *be,* such as *is* and *are.*

## Practice

Circle each title that is incorrect.

1. Brian Lanker is a well-known photographer because of his show and book I dream A world

2. Dorothea Lange was an earlier photographer whose photographs were published in 1939 in her book <u>an american exodus: A Record of Human Erosion</u>

3. Lange's photographs also appeared in the book The Years of bitterness and pride

4. Nate wrote a poem, a study in sadness after seeing Lange's portraits of migrants.

5. Margaret Bourke-White was a news photographer who published books of photographs, including the one titled North of the Danube

6. During her class report on photography, Cassie played The Beautiful blue Danube on the piano.

7. In her story called Go West, young girl, Allison used photographs taken by her favorite nature photographer.

8. Saira decided to use the movie E.T. to report on how movie photographers plan their work.

9. Then she wrote a story called aliens at the movies

Write a sentence for each item below using titles. Be sure to use capital letters, quotation marks, and underlines correctly. **Answers will vary.**

**10.** a song you heard in a movie _____

_____

**11.** a book you have in your desk _____

_____

**12.** a popular song _____

_____

**13.** a poem you read in class _____

_____

**14.** a story everybody knows _____

_____

**15.** the best movie you have ever seen _____

_____

**16.** the title of a book you would like to write _____

_____

**17.** a story in a magazine _____

_____

**18.** a song you can't stand _____

_____

**19.** a book you use in school _____

_____

**20.** a story or essay you have written _____

_____

# Apostrophes

## Learn

**Impressionists'** paintings show real scenes of everyday life.
**They're** mostly of ordinary scenes and ordinary people.

Which boldfaced word shows ownership? _____ Impressionists'

Which boldfaced word combines two words? _____ They're

> To form the **possessive** of a singular noun, add an **apostrophe** and **-s**
> (*an artist's painting*). For plural nouns that end in **s,** add an apostrophe
> (*these artists' styles*). For plural nouns that do not end in **s,** add an
> apostrophe and **-s** (*those women's paintings*). **Apostrophes** are also used
> in **contractions,** two words that have been combined and shortened.

## Practice

Circle the correct word in parentheses. If the answer is a possessive, write **P**. If the answer
is a contraction, write **C**.

1. (Youve/You've) probably read about the art movement known as Impressionism. _____ C

2. These (painters/painters') brushstrokes were sometimes small dots that seemed
   to a viewer like reflected light. _____ P

3. One of this (movements/movement's) artists is Mary Cassatt, who was born
   in Pennsylvania but spent much of her life in France. _____ P

4. Most of (Cassatts'/Cassatt's) paintings are of women and children. _____ P

5. In the painting *The Bath*, she shows a mother washing a (childs'/child's) feet
   in a bowl of water. _____ P

6. (Its/It's) a lovely scene with delicate colors and strong lines. _____ C

7. It shows a warm relationship between the subjects as (theyre/they're) both
   looking down at the water in the bowl. _____ C

8. Cassatt had a way of showing (childrens/children's) positive feelings without
   being sentimental. _____ P

***Strategies for Writers*—Conventions & Skills Practice   Unit 5   95**

# Apply

Rewrite the sentences. Replace the boldfaced words with possessives or contractions.

9. We have seen paintings of water lilies **by Claude Monet**. _____

   We have seen Claude Monet's paintings of water lilies.

10. The paintings **of Monet** were almost all of outdoor scenes. _____

    Monet's paintings were almost all of outdoor scenes.

11. His most famous paintings **did not** have people in them. _____

    His most famous paintings didn't have people in them.

12. **They are** concerned with using light and color to show the scenes. _____

    They're concerned with using light and color to show the scenes.

13. A series of paintings of water lilies is probably the best known of the works of **Monet**.

    A series of paintings of water lilies is probably the best known of Monet's works.

    _____

14. Another of his well-known paintings **is not** of lilies but is of a train station.

    Another of his well-known paintings isn't of lilies but is of a train station.

    _____

15. **It is** an oil painting called <u>Old St. Lazare Station, Paris</u>. _____

    It's an oil painting called <u>Old St. Lazare Station, Paris</u>.

16. Perhaps <u>Impression: Sunrise</u> **should have** been the most famous of his paintings .

    Perhaps <u>Impression: Sunrise</u> should've been the most famous of his paintings.

    _____

17. The name **of the movement** was taken from this painting. _____

    The movement's name was taken from this painting.

18. The influence **of the paintings** has continued to this day. _____

    The paintings' influence has continued to this day.

# Commas in a Series

## Learn

We can take choir, band, or piano in our school's music department.

Underline the three items in a series in the sentence above. Circle the punctuation mark that follows each of the first two items.

> A **series** is a list of three or more words or phrases. **Commas** are used to separate the items in a series. The last comma in a series goes before the word *and* or the word *or*.

## Practice

Add commas where they are needed in these sentences. Cross out commas that should not be there.

1. The voices in the middle school choir are soprano, alto, and tenor.

2. The choir sings patriotic songs, popular songs, and folk songs.

3. It is important for each singer to learn the part, to watch the choir director, and to listen to the other singers.

4. The singers are usually accompanied by Ms. Jones on the violin, Mr. Carmen on the piano, or Dr. McGivern on the clarinet.

5. Our choir director has taught us the importance of posture, breathing, and concentration.

6. All of our songs were written by a famous composer, a new musician, or someone from the music department.

7. My favorite composers are Mozart, Schumann, and Beethoven.

8. Robert Schumann composed beautiful piano pieces, songs, and symphonies.

9. Clara Schumann was a fine pianist, a composer of her own works, and a composer of works included in her husband's music.

10. She is remembered for her compositions, her piano concerts, and her support of her husband's work.

Rewrite each sentence in Marita's letter. Include items in a series in each sentence you write.

**Answers may vary. Possible responses appear below.**

Dear Luke,

**11.** How are your classes in organ? Are your classes in flute and voice going well?

Are your classes in organ, flute, and voice going well?

**12.** I have learned about Clara Schumann. I have also learned about her father Friedrich Wieck and her husband Robert Schumann.

I have learned about Clara Schumann, her father Friedrich Wieck, and her husband Robert Schumann.

**13.** Clara composed piano pieces. She also learned piano pieces by memory. She also played in many concerts.

Clara composed piano pieces, learned piano pieces by memory, and played in many concerts.

**14.** She wrote a piano concerto. She wrote a piano trio. She wrote works for solo piano. She wrote songs for violin and piano.

She wrote a piano concerto, a piano trio, works for solo piano, and songs for violin and piano.

**15.** Clara and Robert wrote music for piano. They both taught music to aspiring musicians. They both influenced other musicians.

Clara and Robert wrote music for piano, taught music to aspiring musicians, and influenced other musicians.

**16.** I'll write more after I do my homework. I also have to eat dinner. I have to practice my piano lessons.

I'll write more after I do my homework, eat dinner, and practice my piano lessons.

Your sister,

Marita

# Commas

## Learn

a. "Rosa, did you say your uncle plays in a mariachi orchestra?" asked Joanne.

b. "Yes, Joanne, he plays the trumpet," answered Rosa.

c. Rosa explained that there are two trumpet players in the group, and there are four violin players.

Circle the name of the person being addressed in sentence **a.**

Underline the word that introduces sentence **b.**

What punctuation mark follows each of these words? _comma_

Draw a box around the conjunction that joins the two

parts of sentence **c.**

What punctuation mark comes before the conjunction? _comma_

> **Commas** mark separations between certain parts of sentences and may also tell a reader where to pause. A comma is used to separate an **introductory word** from the rest of a sentence. It is used to separate **independent clauses** in a **compound sentence**. It is also used to separate a **noun of direct address** from the rest of a sentence. A noun of direct address names a person who is being spoken to.

## Practice

A comma is missing from each sentence. Add the missing comma. Then decide why each comma is needed. Write **I** for introductory word, **C** for compound sentence, or **D** for direct address.

1. "Rosa, what other instruments are in mariachi orchestras?" asked Isabel.   _D_

2. "Well, not all mariachi groups have exactly the same instruments," Rosa replied.   _I_

3. "Say, do you know where the word *mariachi* comes from?" we asked Rosa.   _I_

4. "The word is Mexican-Spanish, and it is from the French word *mariage*," she explained.   _C_

5. We wondered what marriage had to do with a musical group, and we asked Rosa for more explanation.   _C_

6. She told us, "You see, from its earliest history, mariachi music has been played at weddings."   _I_

7. "Oh, that makes sense," we said.   _I_

8. Wow, we loved the sounds of that music!   _I_

Rewrite these sentences so that they include the word in parentheses. Be sure to use commas correctly.

9. We looked for recordings of mariachi music. (and) We found five compact disks at the music store.

   We looked for recordings of mariachi music, and we found five compact disks at the music store.

10. Here are recordings of a famous mariachi group. (Lori) _____

    Lori, here are recordings of a famous mariachi group.

11. It's a group in Mexico. (and) It's called Mariachi Vargas de Tecalitlán.

    It's a group in Mexico, and it's called Mariachi Vargas de Tecalitlán.

12. (Look) I found four recordings of a singer who is called the "Queen of Mariachi."

    Look, I found four recordings of a singer who is called the "Queen of Mariachi."

13. Her name is Lola Beltrán. (and) She performed with great drama and emotion.

    Her name is Lola Beltrán, and she performed with great drama and emotion.

14. (Wow) She was featured in 50 musical motion pictures! _____

    Wow, she was featured in 50 musical motion pictures!

15. Have you heard Mariachi Santa Cecelia, who plays at the San José Flea Market? (Eva)

    Eva, have you heard Mariachi Santa Cecelia, who plays at the San José Flea Market?

16. (Yes) I will hear them again next weekend. _____

    Yes, I will hear them again next weekend.

17. They have twelve musicians. (but) They don't all play every song. _____

    They have twelve musicians, but they don't all play every song.

# Using Semicolons

## Learn

   **a.** Animals make music; at least that's what some human musicians think.

   **b.** One musician writes music of animals, he includes their sounds in his music.

Which sentence separates the two independent clauses with the correct punctuation? ____a.____

> A **semicolon** can be used instead of a comma and a conjunction to separate the **independent clauses** in a compound sentence.

## Practice

Add a semicolon to separate the independent clauses in each sentence.

  **1.** Music is one of the oldest art forms; it is probably as old as human beings themselves.

  **2.** Musical instruments have a very long history; people began making flutes about 12,000 years ago.

  **3.** Making music with the voice is a special human accomplishment; it is also characteristic of animals.

  **4.** We're accustomed to thinking of some animal voices more than others; we think about the varieties of bird songs as many voices.

  **5.** Some animals send messages with sound; a cat's meow and a dog's bark are two examples.

  **6.** One particular modern musician listens to sounds of whales and wolves; he thinks of their sounds as music.

  **7.** He plays music for the animals to hear; he believes they sing back to him.

  **8.** This musician has created many songs that include animals singing; his name is Paul Winter.

  **9.** Winter's composition "Ocean Dream" includes songs of gray whales; the whales' music was the inspiration for the composition.

**10.** In "Wolf Eyes," Paul Winter uses a timber wolf's howl; the wolf sings along with Winter's saxophone at the end.

Match each sentence on the left with a sentence on the right to make a compound sentence. Draw a line to match the sentences. Then rewrite each pair of sentences as a compound sentence. Use a semicolon to separate the independent clauses.

Animals have been popular topics for classical musicians.

Camille Saint-Saëns composed the suite <u>Carnival of the Animals</u>.

The suite is humorous.

Saint-Saëns was a success as a child.

A main character in Mozart's opera <u>The Magic Flute</u> plays an ancient kind of flute.

You might know the ballet <u>Swan Lake</u> by Tchaikovsky.

<u>Help, Help, the Globolinks!</u> is an opera for children by Gian Carlo Menotti.

The globolinks are space-age animals.

The suite includes "The Royal March of the Lion."

There are animals in many classical pieces.

He plays bird songs with it.

He had written several piano compositions by the age of five.

The animals sound playful.

The music is graceful like the movement of swans.

Answers may vary. Likely responses are shown below.

11. Animals have been popular topics for classical musicians; there are animals in many classical pieces.

12. Camille Saint-Saëns composed the suite <u>Carnival of the Animals</u>; the suite includes "The Royal March of the Lion."

13. The suite is humorous; the animals sound playful.

14. Saint-Saëns was a success as a child; he had written several piano compositions by the age of five.

15. A main character in Mozart's opera <u>The Magic Flute</u> plays an ancient kind of flute; he plays bird songs with it.

16. You might know the ballet <u>Swan Lake</u> by Tchaikovsky; the music is graceful like the movement of swans.

17. <u>Help, Help, the Globolinks!</u> is an opera for children by Gian Carlo Menotti; the globolinks are space-age animals.

# Direct and Indirect Quotations

## Learn

a. Ms. Marquez asked us whether we knew the name of the first staged musical that included dancing and a story.

b. Ling said, "I know. It was *Oklahoma!*"

Which sentence, **a.** or **b.**, shows a speaker's exact words? ___b.___
Circle the marks that begin and end the quotation.

> A **direct quotation** is a speaker's exact words. Use **quotation marks** at the beginning and the end of a direct quotation. Begin a direct quotation with a capital letter. Use a comma or end punctuation to separate the speaker's exact words from the rest of the sentence. An **indirect quotation** retells a speaker's words. Do not use quotation marks when the word *that* or *whether* comes before a speaker's words.

## Practice

Add quotation marks, commas, and end marks to direct quotations. Write **I** after each indirect quotation and **D** after each direct quotation. Circle lowercase letters that should be capitalized.

1. Renee said, "my grandparents are taking me to a musical production in New York City."      D

2. "What are you going to see?" Jonathan asked.      D

3. Renee said that she was going to see *Aida*.      I

4. "I thought *Aida* was an opera," said Jorge.      D

5. Renee explained that now it is a musical play on Broadway.      I

6. Jonathan asked, "is it really on Broadway, the street, or just in that area?"      D

7. "Yes, it really is on that street," answered Renee.      D

8. "I've heard of it. It has music by Elton John and lyrics by Tim Rice," said Ling.      D

9. Then we asked whether the play had the same story as the opera.      I

10. Renee said that she thought it did but would tell us after she saw it.      I

# Apply

Answers will vary. Possible responses appear below.

Rewrite these sentences. Change the indirect quotations to direct quotations. Change the direct quotations to indirect quotations. Be sure to use punctuation marks correctly.

11. Ms. Marquez explained that the composer Mozart probably started musical theater with his comic operas.

   Ms. Marquez said, "The composer Mozart probably started musical theater with his comic operas."

12. "Later, the English pair Gilbert and Sullivan wrote operettas that were quite humorous," she continued.

   She said that later the English pair Gilbert and Sullivan wrote operettas that were quite humorous.

13. She said that <u>The Mikado</u> and <u>The Pirates of Penzance</u> were two such operettas.

   She said, "<u>The Mikado</u> and <u>The Pirates of Penzance</u> were two such operettas."

14. "In the United States, Jerome Kern and Oscar Hammerstein II wrote <u>Show Boat</u> together in 1927," Ms. Marquez told us.

   Ms. Marquez told us that in the United States, Jerome Kern and Oscar Hammerstein II wrote <u>Show Boat</u>

   together in 1927.

15. She said that in 1943 Hammerstein teamed with Richard Rodgers to write <u>Oklahoma!</u>

   She said, "In 1943, Hammerstein teamed with Richard Rodgers to write <u>Oklahoma!</u>"

16. "Why do we consider <u>Oklahoma!</u> so important?" asked Mariana.

   Mariana asked why we consider <u>Oklahoma!</u> so important.

17. Our teacher explained that it was the first musical to include a connected story told through singing, dancing, and dialogue.

   Our teacher explained, "It was the first musical to include a connected story told through

   singing, dancing, and dialogue."

**104**  Unit 5  *Strategies for Writers*—Conventions & Skills Practice            Copyright © Zaner-Bloser, Inc.

# Friendly Letters

Dear Sang,

   I am having a great time visiting Aunt Mary. We have been to three shows on Broadway. They all have dancing. You know how much I love to see dancing! I'll tell you all about it in two weeks. Write when you can.

                                    Your friend,
                                    Susan

There are five different parts in this letter. Circle each of the five parts.

> A **friendly letter** has five parts. The **heading** gives the writer's address and the date. The **greeting** includes the name of the person being written to. It begins with a capital letter and ends with a comma. The **body** gives the message. The **closing** is a friendly way to say good-bye. It begins with a capital letter and ends with a comma. The **signature** is the writer's name.

## Practice

Draw a line from the word in the Word Bank to the part of the letter it names.

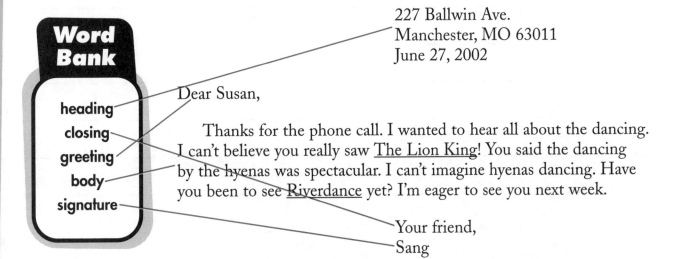

**Word Bank**

heading
closing
greeting
body
signature

227 Ballwin Ave.
Manchester, MO 63011
June 27, 2002

Dear Susan,

   Thanks for the phone call. I wanted to hear all about the dancing. I can't believe you really saw The Lion King! You said the dancing by the hyenas was spectacular. I can't imagine hyenas dancing. Have you been to see Riverdance yet? I'm eager to see you next week.

Your friend,
Sang

# Apply

Write a friendly letter to a friend telling about a musical event you attended. Include a heading, greeting, body, closing, and signature in the correct places. Try to use some of the words in the Word Bank.

## Word Bank

| | | | |
|---|---|---|---|
| vocal | orchestra | movie | lighting |
| dance | concert | folk music | songs |
| favorite part | musical instruments | microphone | applause |

Answers will vary.

_____

_____

_____

_____

_____

_____

_____

_____

_____

_____

_____

_____

_____

# Index of Skills

## Social Studies

geography
> mountains, 57–58
>> Himalayas, 57
>
> rivers, 59–62
>> Mississippi, 61
>> Nile and Amazon, 59
>> other, 60, 62
>
> United States
>> District of Columbia, 18
>> island possessions, 17
>> Mississippi River, 61
>> population, 47–48
>> Route 66, 66

government
> United Nations, 15
> U.S. highway system, 65–66

history, ancient, Western Hemisphere
> Anasazi and Chaco Canyon, 49–51
> Aztec, 21–22

history, United States
> Lewis and Clark, 13–14, 53–54
> Louisiana Purchase, 11–12
> slavery and the Civil War, 19–20
> Spain and the Southwest, 7–8

history, world
> World War II and the Cold War, 25–26
>> Winston Churchill, 23–26

people/places/cultures
> African Americans
>> McKissack, Patricia and Fredrick, 70
>> photographers, 91–93

China: pandas, 37–38

Europe: *Castle,* 80

Latin America, 21–22, 59–60

miscellanea: flags, 9–10, 15–16, 17–18

Native Americans
> Anasazi and Chaco Canyon, 49–51, 53–54
> *Pueblo,* 79

## Science

life science
> agriculture, 63–64
> endangered animals, 37–41
>> alligator (and crocodile), 41–42
>> bald eagle, 39
>> panda, 37–38
>> whooping crane, 40
>
> life expectancy, 43–44

physical science
> astronomy and space exploration, 27–36
> geology: water cycle, 45–46
> weather, 55–56

## Language Arts

children's literature, writers, and illustrators
> *Flossie and the Fox,* 69
> *How to Talk to Your Cat,* 81
> *I-Know-Not-What, I-Know-Not-Where,* 83
> McKissack, Patricia and Fredrick, 70
> *Sun, Moon, and Stars,* 84
> *A Wrinkle in Time,* 68

communication: library technology, 85–86

## Visual and Performing Arts